Advance Review Copy

Uncorrected and not for sale.

ELOPE YOUR LIFE

Cover design: Rebecca Finkel, F + P Graphic Design
Book design: Bryan Tomasovich, The Publishing World
Author photo: Anne Blodgett
Additional photo credits

Starns, Sam
Elope Your Life: A Guide to Living Authentically and Unapologetically, Starting with "I Do"
ISBN 978-0-578-67652-4

Also for sale in ebook format: ISBN TK

1. Reference / Weddings. 2. Travel / Adventure. 3. Self-Help / Personal Growth / Happiness.
4. Family & Relationships / Marriage & Long-Term Relationships. 5. Photography / Celebratons

Distributed by Ingram

Printed in the U.S.A.

ELOPE YOUR LIFE

A Guide to Living
Authentically and Unapologetically,
Starting with "I Do"

SAM STARNS

ELOPE YOUR LIFE

PART ONE: EMPOWERMENT

PART TWO: TO ELOPE OR NOT TO ELOPE

PART THREE: LET'S DO THIS!

TRUE STORIES

PART ONE

EMPOWERMENT

WHY I WISH
I HAD ELOPED

Dreams of princess dresses, long lacy veils, best friends, and flowers everywhere...doesn't every little girl dream of her wedding day? Certainly when we look to popular culture—movies, bridal magazines, and especially advertising—it *seems* that the childhood dream of a "perfect wedding" is universal.

Let me start off by saying that, as a kid, I never dreamed about my wedding. I never even really thought about marrying someone until my husband, Brian, came along. I repeatedly told my now-husband during the planning stages that I was cool with eloping to Maui, where we had previously planned a vacation two months before the wedding.

We're adventurous people by nature and have our own interests that have never exclusively aligned with a particular group. We love theatre, the outdoors, and trying new things. We also love our friends yet we don't have those established groups of friends that one would typically think of when choosing a wedding party.

I tried to reason with myself that having a traditional wedding was what I genuinely wanted. I had lived on the same ranch for my entire childhood and into college. I have a connection to the property and thought, "I could have my wedding here. That would be okay." Brian insisted that a ceremony with the traditional fixings was what he wanted and definitely what his family would want.

The majority of our engagement was spent telling people that we were trying to keep the wedding "small," to about 130 people. Inviting one person meant inviting another in his or her friend circle, and fielding phone calls from Brian's family about why distant family members hadn't been invited.

If the stress of planning a wedding wasn't enough, the day itself brought so many problems, some of which were six months in the making. So, let's break down the mistakes I made that came to fruition on our wedding day—all of these reaffirmed why I wish I had eloped.

I didn't even have a "day of" coordinator.

You would think that, after photographing weddings, I would apply what I had learned to my own wedding. Nope. I was the one running between vendors, making sure everything was getting done. The first dance? I made sure that happened by working with our DJ (who was, in the middle of all of this, fabulous). Same with the father-daughter dance. Time spent managing things (most of which I'll cover): almost all damn day. Time spent during the reception with my husband, not including the first dance: five minutes.

And that was when we were eating.

My venue was my parents' ranch.

While it was free, it came with its own challenges. At an all-inclusive venue, you don't have to worry about setup or takedown. My friends and family helped set up, but guess who was left to take down the tables and chairs, and stack the dirty dishes? My new husband, along with one of the groomsmen, and me still in my wedding makeup and hair-do. A few of the guests felt terrible when they saw us and joined in to help. I was so embarrassed.

My poor aunt, and my poor mother.

To save on catering at our rurally-located ranch, my aunt (who is an amazing cook) offered to cook some savory comfort food. It was delicious, but my aunt couldn't savor the day as a guest and honored family member. Also, my mother: I found out later that she didn't enjoy the day because she was so busy trying to manage things.

"You HAVE TO invite Aunt Carol!"

Okay, I don't actually have an Aunt Carol, but in the months leading up to our wedding, I got *so much* flack from people about whom I should or should not invite. This was probably the single factor that most influenced my wish that Brian and I had eloped.

I had calls from family members pressuring me to invite people who had flaked out on me during some of the most significant moments of my life. I also had some people call my husband and end up nosing their way into an invitation because Brian is the nicest person on the planet. We were told we must invite a distant uncle from Brian's family whom I had never met. We tried to get contact information through multiple channels, and finally decided we had made enough of an effort and gave up the search for him. A few months before the wedding, Brian received an upset phone call from the uncle asking why he hadn't been invited.

I even had some future in-laws bring uninvited guests whom I had never met. They did this despite the fact that we had explained multiple times that we didn't have the room or the budget for additional guests. That led to a minor scene as place cards were handed out and in turn, kicked some people—including my soon-to-be mother-in-law!—out of their seats.

The dance floor was divided.

When you are #blessed (in this case, I admit to using this hashtag with some irony) with friends from so many different walks of life, it's hard to get them to mesh. I line dance, and I also have a lot of theatre friends who prefer things like Broadway show tunes, and fun songs like "Time Warp." Both sides kept requesting songs, and it was hard to combine those, and some guests left early because they weren't able to participate on the dance floor. Sure, there were more pressing problems than this, but it nonetheless left us feeling even more overwhelmed and, in the end, disheartened.

On top of everything else, some of the guests showed up more than an hour early! Brian and I were right in the middle of having our wedding photographs taken. What should have been an intimate moment, when Brian and I shared our "first look," was instead remarkably awkward because we had an audience of early arrivers chatting while they watched us. It sounded like a few even made jokes at my expense. I felt like I was on stage in a play I definitely did not write.

The weather was spotty for an outdoor gathering of that magnitude. The amount of leftover food and drink (we had determined how much alcohol to buy with one of those online calculators) was substantial. We were left with more than half of the alcohol we had purchased. All of that had to go home with somebody.

But most dispiriting, I realized that I was doing all of this *to please other people*. I was responding to some of the things I had heard during our six-month engagement:

"My parents would be hurt if we didn't have a ceremony."

"You're TOTALLY inviting me to your wedding, right?"

"Fine, if you don't invite them, I'm not coming."

"You don't have to invite so-and-so, but if they inquire, I want you to go ahead and say they can come."

We ended up spending money on things we no longer have or have since forgotten. We spent money on decor, food, and pleasing *other people* when the day should have been more about Brian and myself.

About two months before our wedding, Brian, who was by then helping out so much with the wedding plans, turned to me and asked, "Is it too late to elope?"

I said yes, it was too late because we had so many non-refundable retainers out in the world. I learned later that there's a name for this madness: "the sunk cost fallacy." The idea is that if you have already spent a lot of time or money on something, you are more likely to carry on, even if it's not the best thing for you. This can play out as something like, "We've already spent $5,000 on deposits, we may as well spend another $20,000 on the wedding, even if it's not what we had really, truly hoped for." Looking back, that's a pretty sad reason to go through with something about which you and your partner are not wildly enthusiastic. My preference would have been to elope to Maui or some other epic place and invite a handful of people whom we truly wanted to be there with us.

Do you know what happened after the wedding? Brian and I went home and I cried. And not happy tears.

I knew then that the most important thing I missed out on was celebrating the connection between my husband and me. If we had taken a bold step and done something that was radically different on *our* day, we could have enjoyed a sense of true connection and celebration. Looking back, I didn't have people eloping and

sharing on social media about their phenomenal experience. In my small, conservative hometown, I didn't know anyone who had done anything close to eloping. It was all barn weddings with mason jars, hay bales, lace, and burlap.

I didn't have bold, confident people to look to when I was planning my wedding. I didn't realize the day could be about my husband and me and who we are together instead of this misguided, societally mandated duty that doesn't fit every relationship. And, while some may disagree, a wedding is about the couple and their commitment; it is not about anyone who thinks they have a right to be invited.

Something Else I Should Not Have Done...

...is look at those ridiculous wedding boards on the internet. You know the ones I'm talking about, right? Most of those boards are set up for brides to judge each other on superficial things (really, who has a $7,000 restroom towed in for guests?). On some of these boards, opinions on elopements and intimate weddings can be dismissive or even downright cruel.

But those opinions don't matter.

With all that said, I'm here to say this: *you do you*. If you want to have a gorgeous, huge wedding with all the trimmings, go for it! But don't be discouraged or pressured into something like that if it isn't representative of who you and your partner are.

*

I believe that you will find something magical in the process of *you doing you*. If that turns out to be an adventure elopement, I can tell you that it will change your life. There is so much to discover in the process: being intentional as you design one of the most personal and powerful experiences for you and the person whom you have chosen to marry. When you create something that is entirely you, not dictated by tradition or fashion, it can be life-changing. The experience becomes a part of you.

And why stop at your wedding day? Why not *elope your life*? We'll explore taking that jump to complete freedom in the form of *you doing you* across all aspects of your life.

This is such an exciting journey and I am honored to share it with you.

THERE IS
ONLY ONE YOU

"All the elements in your body were forged many many millions of years ago in the heart of a faraway star that exploded and died. That explosion scattered those elements across the desolations of deep space. After so, so many millions of years, these elements came together to form new stars and new planets. And on and on it went. The elements came together and burst apart, forming shoes and ships and sealing wax and cabbages and kings. Until, eventually, they came together to make you. You are unique in the universe."

—Doctor Who

You are a singular event in the timeline of the universe.

There is not another person on Earth like you. There never has been and there never will be. Your specific set of experiences makes you unlike anyone else. Think about all of the dreams you have pursued, the struggles you've overcome, and the life that you have created. All of that being said, why would you think you could compare yourself to someone else? Why would you, a unicorn, compare yourself to a mermaid?

You have lived an amazing story full of struggles and triumphs. It's hard to see that when society is telling you that you've got to be the best, that you've got to be at the top. Instagram reminds us every day that we are not beautiful enough, not wealthy enough, not liked enough, that we don't have what it takes to "go viral" (I wonder how long the definition of *that* will last).

Oh, social media, how you taunt us! You show us snapshots. You are run by an algorithm that curates stories already curated by the people who post them. You show us a perfect life that doesn't exist in reality. And we "follow" and "favorite" and wonder what went wrong in our own lives.

I could offer example after example, but it's likely going to take you sitting down and really thinking about it. That's what it took for me. I was speaking with my mentor, and it just came out of my mouth. I didn't even realize what I was saying until I was already saying it: "I wish every person deeply understood that they cannot compare who they are and what they do to anyone else in the world." It just can't be done. It's not fair to either person.

It took me a long, long time to see that, though. And do you know what? It's still a struggle. If I'm honest, I still occasionally find myself comparing what I've done to others' accomplishments and thinking that I somehow missed the boat. It can be comparing myself to others' recognition, or accomplishments, or talents. I could have done so much better, I tell myself... I could have been so much more. But then I remind myself that I've got to run my own race and do the best that I can do. Because that's all that I can ask of myself.

And what about you? Do you know what sets you apart from everyone else? This is going to take some time. We are complicated and complex creatures. Think about these aspects of yourself and also your partner.

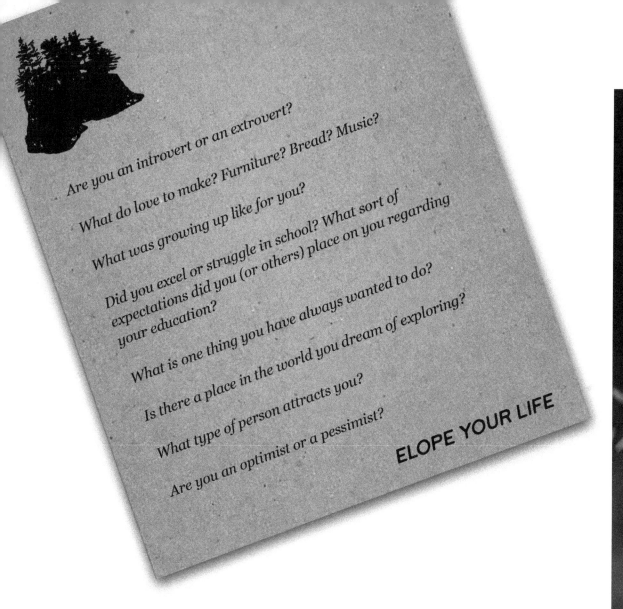

Are you an introvert or an extrovert?

What do love to make? Furniture? Bread? Music?

What was growing up like for you?

Did you excel or struggle in school? What sort of expectations did you (or others) place on you regarding your education?

What is one thing you have always wanted to do?

Is there a place in the world you dream of exploring?

What type of person attracts you?

Are you an optimist or a pessimist?

ELOPE YOUR LIFE

I could go on and on. We live in such busy times that it has become rare to sit down and really think about questions like these.

From here, if you're reading this and have a significant other (I suspect if you're thinking about eloping, you've got one of those), think about your commonalities. What brought you two together? Do you have the same sense of humor? Do you like the same activities? Are both of you travel junkies? Did you go through something together as friends that led your friendship to evolve into something more?

Write down a list of what makes you unique as a couple. No other couple is exactly like the two of you together. So, why would you decide to have a wedding or do anything in life that doesn't reflect you both? There are so many blogs, articles, forums, and groups—not to mention magazines and television shows—telling you what you should and shouldn't do concerning your wedding. But how can they be an authority on your wedding without

even knowing you? They can't. So don't listen to them. I made the mistake of doing just that, and I regret my wedding. I know so many others who feel the same way:

> *"We really didn't want to have to juggle the opinions of everyone from both of our big families throughout the planning process, and we didn't want anyone to influence our day."*

"We have always felt more comfortable and happy outdoors and exploring. We know that there are a million outdoor venues but we really wanted to feel nature on our day, not just use it as a backdrop."

"We both have been nomadic due to our work for the past few years, and while that satisfies our gypsy souls, it has made us very selfish with our time together."

You can't honestly tell me that the people who said these things fit into a cookie-cutter wedding or marriage setup. They felt the same way. So they decided to make their wedding day reflect their lives together. Which is pretty bold, in my opinion.

When you've finally decided, "Yes, we're going to have a wedding day that fits us," it's time to think about what you want to include. Think about what you enjoy doing together. Think about your traditions (remember, traditions come in all shapes and sizes; they don't just involve putting a tree up together on Christmas). Is it time to make a new tradition? Your wedding day is a perfect opportunity to experience something new.

This is where "nothing is impossible" comes in.

I have had couples who love animals. So the few human guests they invited were also welcome to bring their pets. There are couples who had always wanted to go on a helicopter ride, so they hired a charter and took in the sights while in their wedding attire. I've hiked into a ceremony location before dawn at Glacier National Park. I have met a couple at sunset near the Villa Borghese in Rome. I have traveled with couples to places like Kauai so they could start their marriage with a tropical honeymoon and a horseback ride.

I am going to encourage you to dream. Really dream. Expenses, location, and other logistics be damned. If there were no compromises made, what would be your dream for your wedding day? You can include traditional wedding moments like a "first look," or getting ready images, and also nontraditional things like a non-white wedding dress, matching tattoos, helicopter rides, snorkeling, hiking, a picnic, horseback riding... the list is endless. Think about what you'd like to see and do on your wedding day. What comes to mind?

Consider this: I didn't have someone to look to when I wanted to elope, but instead was planning my traditional wedding. I didn't have Instagram or websites dedicated to couples eloping. There were offbeat weddings, but none were really what I was looking for. If I had seen couples eloping and websites and books with insights on how to elope and the empowering message that it was okay, I think our wedding would have turned out very differently.

Today, I get to work with the couples whom I wish I had around during my engagement. I lovingly refer to them as "my couples" because this experience brings us together in a special way. And these couples? What they are doing takes courage and confidence. They are 100 percent being themselves.

People always say that they want to make a difference. The urge to leave on Earth something tangible, something lasting to confirm you existed, is a pretty strong feeling. But the quickest way to make a difference in even one life is to be yourself. By being confident in themselves and their decisions on their marriage and wedding, my couples and so many others are inspiring people by simply doing what they genuinely want to do. And it doesn't take getting married to do this. Be yourself. Show up the way you want to show up, be confident about your likes and dislikes. That confidence is contagious. It gives others the courage to be themselves, too. If you can be unapologetically yourself, you can inspire others to be who they are.

What better effect to have on the world than being who we are?

DON'T LET ANYONE PRESSURE YOU

OUT OF BEING SPECTACULAR

Once you embrace the truth, that you are absolutely spectacular—the only *you* in the universe—good things will begin to happen. For me, realizing that I was already "enough" changed so many things, both big and small. I'm not sure how much other people noticed the changes. But do you know what? That doesn't matter.

Since I've accepted the fact that I'm unique and that I can't compare myself to anyone else, I've become more productive. It's incredible how much time I had spent comparing myself to others instead of actually getting things done. Now? I'm keeping up my gym routine, I'm devoting more time to my couples, I'm even becoming more organized (my mother is probably throwing her hands up in frustration thinking back to my childhood bedroom).

More importantly, I've become happier. Theodore Roosevelt said that comparison is the thief of joy, and boy, is that ever true. I sort of believed it before, but ever since "the moment" with my mentor, I deeply believe it. Those peers who are viral on Instagram,

those former classmates who look like they've got it all together, the brides in the bridal magazines, they don't affect me the way they did before. And that is such a good thing because there's this feeling of anxiety that happens when you compare yourself to others: it's one part fear mixed with equal parts low self-esteem and fixation or obsession. Becoming free of that is like having a dark cloud lifted from your life.

Once I broke free from comparing myself to others, I could see more clearly that I have, in fact, been a risk-taker. I have found myself in situations where I thought, "That's cool. I want to try that!" and then I did. Sometimes I felt like a natural. Other times required... ahem... more practice. But ultimately, my willingness to take things on led me to get involved in a garden club, 4-H, pony club, to be an announcer for a high-end dressage show, perform in theatre, pick up different instruments, snowboard, learn new languages, live abroad, start a new business, take ballet, and organize an effort to illuminate my local downtown with Christmas lights during the holidays. It's not that everything was effortless; I struggled, I dealt with depression, I had some bad relationships before I met Brian. But the fact that it hadn't all been easy should have given me more confidence that I could accomplish anything, no matter how difficult.

So, looking back, when I wanted to elope, why did I not think it was possible? I jokingly say that I wanted to elope and my husband wanted a traditional wedding. So we compromised. And had a wedding. I often roll my eyes when I tell that story. Because about a month and a half before the wedding, I finally enrolled Brian in helping with the planning. He quickly realized that he wanted to elope, too. At that point, I felt it was too late to cancel. In hindsight (and speaking with others who were involved), it wouldn't have been surprising to anyone if we *had* chosen to throw all our nonrefundable retainers down the toilet and elope. And really, I wish we had.

What was wrong with me? This gal who never seemed to think anything was impossible. What happened? I'll tell you: societal pressure happened. Family pressure happened. I got in *my own way*. I thought so much about what other people wanted and expected that, even with my newfound sense of uniqueness, I got a bit lost.

Silly Sam. Over the past several years I've become more aware of what I didn't have when planning for my wedding. I didn't have *empowerment*. Sure, I had a best friend mention that I should say "screw it" and elope. But it was one friend against all my wedding guests and some people who weren't even invited (but showed up anyway!). At the time, I didn't know how I could go about eloping but still maintain that wedding day feeling. I didn't have the stories and experiences of others to assure me that I would be making the best decision for me, and for me and Brian as a couple.

I let family and societal pressure crush my spectacular self.

FINDING

YOUR BALANCE

Praise. It's like a verbal or written form of a pat on the head. We love to hear when we are doing well; it gives us a mini high of sorts. Think back on teachers, coaches, or (if you are a theatre person), directors who said, "You did a great job." Can you still feel that rush of happiness, even years later? A friend of mine recounted how her dance teacher would tell her students, "You weren't good... You were excellent." That's praise, and it feels wonderful.

Praise can lead us to push ourselves harder because we love how praise feels, or we love the person who is giving it. Some of people's best work happens when they are being praised for what they do. As I write this, I am thinking about Jerry from the Netflix docuseries "Cheer." Anyone who wouldn't want a "mat talk" and some praise from him obviously is just crazy. (If you don't know who Jerry is, put this book down right now and look up "Jerry Harris Mat Talk.") If being praised can help us push ourselves to achieve our goals, it must be a good thing, right?

Then there's the opposite of the mat talk: praise that, rather than lifting you up, has a twinge of putting you in what others consider "your place," or at least the place that makes them feel most comfortable. Ouch.

"Oh my gosh you look so stunning in that Cinderella-style wedding gown."

But what if you had your heart set on a beaded boho mermaid style dress with a kickass cape? You know that's the wedding dress you've always dreamt of, but now your mom and bridesmaids are making you feel guilty for not being as in love with the fairytale ball gown as they are. So what do you do? You sigh and put your dream dress back on the rack since everyone else is tearing up over the Cinderella dress.

"Your aunt and uncle still talk about how much fun they had at your graduation party and they can't wait for your wedding."

Of course everyone loves a good wedding! Great music, good food, even better company. What people often forget is the financial, familial, and emotional stress it puts on the very couple the day is meant to be celebrating. You love your aunt and uncle—and your cousins, your friends, your extended family, your neighbors, the random people your parents go to church with whose names you don't even know, the kids you grew up babysitting, and the person you used to go to school with back in 4th grade whom you bumped into at a coffee shop and who basically invited herself—don't you? So obviously you're going to put aside your emotional well-being and throw an elaborate party, right?

"You're so brilliant at science and mathematics, it would be a shame if you ever stopped teaching."

You have aced every math quiz you've ever taken, in fact, it comes to you more naturally than the English language. Science is something you enjoy because it's like a puzzle you need to figure out; however, your true passion is motivational speaking. When someone tells you that doing or wearing or choosing something you love is "a shame," it can sound (to your soul) like "Why in the world would you chase your passion when you could just settle and make other people happy?"

Why should you spend your life trying to please people? It's simple: you shouldn't. If your whole life is only about trying to please people, you will eventually be miserable—and I mean the falling flat on your face, with skinned-up knees and carpet burn on your palms, wind-knocked-out-of-you kind of miserable. Why? Because it is 100% impossible to please everyone all of the time. Read that sentence again. Not going back to read it? Okay, fine. It is 100 percent impossible to please everyone all of the time.

Hell, if you aren't making someone upset, you're not doing it right!

Do not try to please people with your major life decisions. If you let others dictate any and every choice you make, there's a huge chance you could live with years of hurt, regret, and what ifs, because you didn't take control of your own life.

You may be thinking, "Sam, you're being dramatic. That doesn't happen."

Really? Tell that to the girl who picked an in-state college that her parents were pushing even though her dream was a thousand miles away at an SEC university. Sure she graduated from her in-state school with honors, yet she asks herself that "what if" question every single day.

There is a huge difference between praise and manipulation.

There is nothing wrong with wanting people to cheer you on and praise your decisions. It's natural. We want to make people happy. The point when it becomes manipulation is when the decision causes you harm in order to keep others appeased. Your mental health, emotional health, physical health, spiritual health, and financial health should never have to take a blow to the gut just to keep people around you happy. For example:

Why are you having a wedding?

"Because I'm the baby of the family, and neither of my siblings had a traditional wedding so it's what's expected of me."

Manipulation.

"Because I've dreamt of having all my best friends there to celebrate alongside me as we dance the night away."

Healthy.

ELOPE YOUR LIFE

Why are you staying in that career that you hate?

"Because my boss said he doesn't know how his business could stay open if I left."

Manipulation.

"Because I'm waiting a few months until my finances are in order so I can make the switch in a way that won't cause unnecessary financial or personal stress."

Healthy.

Something beautiful happens when you take the reins of your life. You find a place where you can give back to others in a holistic and meaningful way. When you have decided that you might need to take a step back from the local HOA board or let Lisa run the bake sale committee (since she's always implying you don't know how to run the damn thing, anyway) you may suddenly find yourself with free time. GASP! You might be able to pursue those passions, take that class, open that business, and spend time with your family. And what happens from there? Once you take that class you realize you have a real talent at making pottery. Once you open that business you realize

you are serving your community in a much more meaningful and lasting way than you ever could have while making decisions about shrubbery in HOA meetings. Once you spend more time with your family, you realize you are able to communicate better, build bonds with those who matter to you, and your relationships flourish and become stronger than ever. When I say "family," I don't mean the stereotypical 1950s family with 2.5 children and a dog. You and your spouse are a family before you have kids, *if you even decide to have kids*. You are a family if it's just you and a few roommates, or if it's you and a community of like-minded people with whom you consciously surround yourself. "Family" is what you create. You get to choose.

When you focus on yourself, pursue the things that are healthy for you, and serve people in a way that doesn't leave you feeling like you're on low-power mode, you can find your balance. You won't need to be a people-pleaser because you'll know that you are already enough, without bending to what other people think. You might be surprised (and some people around you will definitely be surprised) by the power you'll find in being authentically you—and that's the groundwork for *eloping your life*.

5

WHAT ELOPING IS
TO ME

To me, eloping is not about the photos.
I am guessing that you are thinking "What? An adventure elopement photographer who thinks eloping isn't about the photos?" Stay with me for a minute. *Eloping is about a transformation that is the catalyst for real change for the rest of your life.* Think about all the defining moments in your life so far. There were moments that edified you. There were dreadful moments that ultimately were life-changing. Think about those moments when you had to be strong and fight and you came out on the other side, completely changed.

That is what eloping can be and that is what I want to do for you. Often, the defining moments in our lives, those that change us, and shape us, and make us into the person we are meant to be, come from doing things and experiencing things outside of our comfort zone. Two of the most defining moments in my life were when I lived and studied abroad and

when I realized I could help others create change in their lives through eloping. Were those comfortable all of the time? No.

Living abroad taught me an entirely new level of respect for another culture. It was tough being away from my family, with a host family to whom I did not feel connected. I went into the experience thinking it would be one thing, and it was nearly the opposite. However, I learned so much about myself: that I could handle being isolated, that I could explore on my own, and that no matter how far away I am from everything I know, I can survive.

A few years later, right before Brian and I got married, I found out that my position as a paralegal had been made redundant. This forced me to consider my career options. It was the catalyst for me to go into photography full-time. It is safe to say I wouldn't be where I am today had the law firm not decided to restructure my position.

EMPOWERMENT

Those defining moments didn't change me completely, but they did make me a more complex and more genuine version of myself. Eloping can do that. Most likely, it won't be entirely easy. You will face potential disagreements, backlash, stress, and so much more, but in the end, your thoughts, desires, dreams, and wishes are valid and worth pursuing. Especially the ones that scare you. Any time you feel uncomfortable or worried, know that what you're fearful of is likely exactly the thing you should take on.

What if your life had no self-imposed limits? What if you could suddenly do the things that made you feel scared or nervous, or that you simply thought you couldn't manage? What if you discovered new insights about yourself in the process? Imagine traveling to a new location and experiencing the amazing scenery, while discovering that you can navigate big city traffic when that normally sends you into an anxiety spiral. What if you developed a newfound love for dressing up (maybe a date to the opera or theatre is in your future!) to look your best just for yourself and your spouse. Maybe you unearth the strength to stand up for your wishes with family and friends. How great could that be? Becoming more confident in your abilities? Reviving a love of yourself and how you look? Discovering a new power of being a spectacular advocate for yourself? Who wouldn't want to expand mentally and emotionally? Even if you can't admit it to yourself, I'm shouting from the rooftops. *I* want you to be the absolute best version of yourself. I'm rooting for your development and continual growth! I want you to grow with your partner and I want your relationship to get better and closer every single day.

This could also be a time when you and your partner intentionally sit down and talk about new wishes and dreams that you can accomplish together. Taking that time to sit and reflect is a great exercise to do together or separately. Everyone is so busy keeping up and trying to survive in an increasingly fast-paced world that it's not often we have an opportunity to update our consciousness on new dreams and interests, and even to consider facets of life we may have grown tired of. An elopement season is an opportunity to allow yourself to grow.

This season of your life is full of tests. You can either choose to take an easier route or to stand up for yourself and your relationship. And when you choose not to take an easier way out, you are simply left with one option: to become a better and stronger version of you. The quote should be "necessity is the mother of all growth" instead of "invention."

Eloping is about so much more than a ceremony and great photos. The entire process can help shape you into who you are meant to be. It's about doing the thing that speaks to you the most, that uncovers facets of your being.

Do you want to know yourself more completely? That's what elopement can do for you, and I want to help you accomplish it.

ELOPING AS A
TRANSFORMATION

I'm not here to empower you as much as I'm here to help *you* unearth the power that you already have inside. Often, people don't realize how strong they are until they are faced with an obstacle that requires them to give it all they have. Eloping is a perfect place to begin that discovery of the strength you are made of.

Whether you've been dreaming about your wedding since you were little or (more likely) haven't thought about it a lot, it is common knowledge that wedding planning can test the limits and sanity of even the most serene person. There are travel logistics to consider, details to organize, vendors to book, and friends and family who will have questions.

The part that I have seen require the most strength is dealing with other people. I get it. We don't want to hurt the ones we care about most. But at some point, choose yourself. "Conscious selfishness" is the awareness that, in order to give your best self to others, you first might have to say no to some things (or people) that don't bring you happiness. That means allocating time to relax, scheduling personal time, and yes, doing things that ignite excitement within you. And on one of the biggest days of your life? That is as good a time as any to practice conscious selfishness.

You might start out wanting an adventurous elopement for the "pretty factor," as I call it. I don't blame you. It looks fun, romantic, and exciting. But here is the thing: it can be so much more. Eloping can be a transformation that flows into the rest of your life. You discover things about yourself—what you like, dislike, how far you can be pushed, and what really moves you, among other things. Undoubtedly, you will go through trials. Your family and friends may question your decision. You might get stuck on logistics or disagree with your partner about who is invited. There is still some planning involved, so the process of putting everything together can be stressful. You might also have to think critically about what you want out of your day. How will the two of you focus on your connection and the experience around you without getting distracted by all the hubbub of the wedding industry and what Aunt Carol thinks is best?

I believe that most, if not all, life-changing experiences are not easy. They are hard. They push and pull you across a spectrum of emotions. You'll feel frustrated, scared, excited, nervous, and lost. But what happens next? You overcome. You change. You evolve. You become a more complex person because of that experience. You become who you were meant to be.

Your thoughts, ideas, and dreams are valid. They are worth pursuing.

Sometimes it takes a watershed moment in your life for you to realize you need to take a stand for what you believe in or want with all your being. For most of my couples, their watershed moment was their wedding. They didn't want other people dictating how things needed to go on one of the most important days of their lives. They wanted to take that moment and transform it into something truly beautiful and uniquely them. When their mother-in-law started insisting that every single extended family member be invited and be granted plus-ones, it was a wakeup call that things had spiraled out of control and they needed to grab the reins of their wedding and relationship, they needed to reclaim it, and they needed to elope.

My couples often find out so much more about each other, their character, their hopes, and dreams when they choose to elope. They are making huge moves together for the first time, establishing what their marriage will be from day one. The process transforms them from a couple who is trying to please everyone else to a couple who is firm and secure in their decisions. They go from a couple worried about whether they can even afford the honeymoon if they offer three meal choices to their guests to a couple who can quite literally start their honeymoon off from the moment they say "I do," because you can elope in some pretty amazing locations. They go from worrying about what others will think about them, to thinking about themselves and setting a firm foundation for their future. It sets them up for success, and it can set you up for success.

This is a moment in your life when you will learn to stop living according to other peoples' expectations of you if those expectations don't fit your own wants, needs, and standards. There are other moments in life where people have the same realization and transformation. A son or daughter who doesn't want to go into medicine as their parents urge him or her to do has a choice to make. Does the son or daughter live for their parents or live for themselves? Eloping is another time when you have to make such a decision. Do you want the day that is based on your

commitment to one another to be about the two of you? Or do you want it to be about the wants and needs of everyone around you? Wanting other people to be happy is not a bad thing, but I believe there must be a balance. And eloping? That is about making yourselves happy.

At the end of your elopement journey, you will likely have gained so much more than a spouse and great memories. You will surely have gained some courage, strength, and knowledge that you can harness and utilize, whether that is by sharing, educating and inspiring others, or relying on that strength in your own life. How so? The possibilities are limited only by you. Do something new. Change your routines or even your career.

It would be a shame to discover more of yourself in this process and then discard it. In fact, I am not sure you could. It would be difficult, if not impossible, to not be affected by the experience of eloping. So why not consciously make the decision to harness that?

Eloping your life starts with eloping. So that is where we will begin here, as well. I want you to have a day that is intentional and unique to you. Doing that requires some preparation and encouragement. That is where the next section comes in. You are going to elope your life. It begins with planning your elopement.

PART TWO

TO ELOPE
OR
NOT TO ELOPE

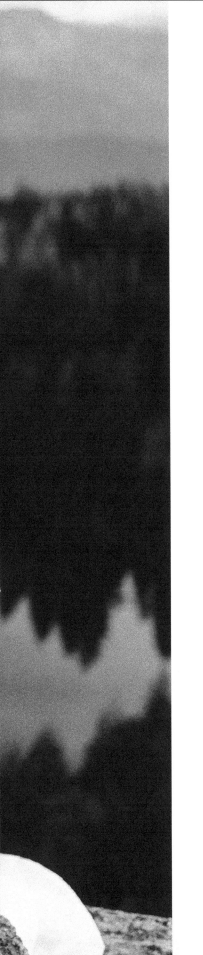

7

SO YOU WANT
TO ELOPE

I have couples tell me all the time, "We wish we could elope" or "We would elope if we could" or some version of that phrase. I can only respond with a question: *What is stopping you?* The reasons people typically give include family drama, expectations, or something similar. The reasons almost never include anything else. It's always about the expectations of family and friends and not wanting to disappoint or displease anyone.

Weddings so quickly become about everyone else except the people who are getting married. I hate to break it to your family and friends, but your wedding should not be about them. A wedding is about uniting two souls, so they may spend the rest of their lives together. It's not about whether

Aunt Carol gets seated far away from the DJ, or whether cousin Debra has a completely vegan and gluten-free meal. It *is* about two people choosing to craft a life together. And when you think about it, this is your day. This is not anyone else's day. It stands to reason that no one has a right to make you do anything you don't want to do on your wedding day.

So, I ask again, what is stopping you? Is it friends? Is it family? Is it the fear of letting someone down? Is it worrying about not including everyone who might want to come, even if you don't want them to be there? All those reasons hinge on other people and what they want. I've never heard a couple say, "We wish we could elope, but physically we can't." Instead, it has always been about not being able to elope because of someone else's expectations—expecting you to have a certain type of wedding, a certain number of guests, and expecting themselves to be invited. It's always about someone else.

After all is said and done, you will be the one with the memories of your special day. Will your friends and family remember the details that you worked so hard to get just right? Will they remember exactly how well the entrée matched the side dishes? Are they going to remember the intricacies of your décor? Probably not. It is crazy to me how so many friends and families have such strong opinions on things like a wedding "theme" when it's *not their wedding*.

Here's the thing: most of the time, people's expectations of you are not the same as your expectations of yourself. No one knows you like you do. And if an intimate wedding with just a few of your close family members and friends or an elopement by yourselves in someplace beautiful and special to you is your speed and your type of wedding, then family, friends, and people who truly love you would not want to hinder that. Other people's concepts of your wedding should not be the reason that you "can't" elope. If anything, those family and friends who love you and care the most about you will be happy that you are doing something that speaks to you and your relationship.

What your friends and family really think about eloping....

I conducted an anonymous survey of nearly 100 people, and more than 60 percent of those surveyed associated the words "adventure" "freedom" & "romance" with the word "elopement." Other top contenders were "fun" and "intentional." More than 90 percent of those surveyed had only positive things to say. When I asked them to describe their definition of an elopement in a sentence, here is what some respondents wrote:

"Elopement is incredibly special and something that truly belongs to the two of you."

"An intimate moment with the person you love to signify the rest of your lives."

"Elopement is making a wedding and a commitment all about you and your relationship, in the most honest, authentic way possible."

"Freedom from the standardization and societal dictation on what lawful commitment means."

ELOPE YOUR LIFE

CULTIVATING

COMPROMISE

A noteworthy question that individuals bring to me is: What if my significant other doesn't want to elope? Let's walk through that. I will usually ask:

"Can she pinpoint what she doesn't like about eloping?"

"Does he want a big party where he is the center of attention?"

"Is it the lack of family being present that's the issue?"

"Is it something else?"

If your partner is unsure about elopement, it's important to identify the aspects of an elopement that make him or her feel uneasy. Then you can begin to work toward a compromise. I mean hey, that's what marriage is going to be like, right?

If the idea of family not being present is concerning, consider a compromise with a few select family members. Many couples have anywhere from two to 20 close family and friends witnessing their vows in a less traditional venue, like a beach or a mountain. That way, there are loved ones present but not so many that it starts requiring seating, a more conventional venue, and all the other trappings of a traditional wedding.

What about the lack of a big ol' party? Listen, I get it. I can do the Cupid Shuffle with the best of them, but it's not everyone's taste. It certainly wasn't my taste for my wedding (though I insisted on having line dancing for all my line-dancing friends). Have you considered eloping and having a honeymoon, then when you return from your trip, hosting a larger reception-like party? You can even wear your wedding attire to the reception. If you prefer a send-off party, remember that it doesn't have to be the day or night before you leave for your ceremony. You are creating new traditions, right? A send-off soirée is a fabulous reason to buy that fierce outfit you've had your eye on. These types of events are becoming more and more common as a way to include loved ones, but still have an intimate experience and adventure on the day you actually get married.

There are also ways to include family members without them actually being present. Bring to the discussion the idea of using technology to include them via FaceTime so they can witness the ceremony without being physically present. Try suggesting that you record a video and have your family be the first to see it. Request letters that you can read during your ceremony or throughout the wedding day.

Sit down together and figure out where you can meet in the middle with an elopement. And remember, the definition of elopement is changing. It doesn't need to be all or nothing. Elopement can mean the two of you getting married unbeknownst to anyone, or it can mean traveling to a destination with a few close friends and family to celebrate your marriage in a way that breaks with tradition.

What if my partner and I can't agree on a location or vibe for our day?

I've been to and researched countless places on this blue globe, and if one of you wants mountains and the other wants oceans for your backdrop, there is a way and a place that combines them. It may take a little searching, but that is where a good planner or elopement photographer who specializes in adventure can swoop in and make life so much easier for you. Personally, I love helping couples discover locations that make both people happy—including places that neither of them may have thought of or known about. Imagine holding your ceremony in Glacier National Park, with its towering glacial peaks and thundering waterfalls. Perhaps the 2,000-year-old Redwoods feel like "home" for your marriage ceremony, with the rugged Oregon Coast just minutes away. You can find ancient mountain peaks and tropical beaches coexisting in places like Hawaii, or see castle ruins before a quick jaunt to colossal sea cliffs and columnar basalt formations in Ireland and Scotland. I can find any combination of landscapes internationally or domestically.

Ultimately, there are ways to reach an understanding when it comes to choosing where to elope. Kevin McCloud, a British designer and environmentalist, wrote that "Life involves other people and it is a compromise." While that's certainly true, I tend to think the hallmark of a good compromise is that both parties are equally satisfied and represented.

IS ELOPING THE

RIGHT CHOICE?

I imagine that just about every couple has considered eloping at some point during the wedding planning process... For my friend Maddie, it was the night she got engaged and her mom handed her a 300-person guest list. For others, it's simply because they want the moment to be immortalized between only the two of them or perhaps a small handful of people whom they care about most in this world.

Why should you elope? Well, because unlike my friend Maddie, you won't have to decide who gets a plus-one even though they're going to break up with their plus-one a month after the wedding. You won't have to cry over the fact that the reception venue costs $65 a plate. You won't have to spend hours selecting the "right" fonts for your invitations, RSVPs, and place cards. You won't have to choose between live flowers and the dream dress you've had in mind.

An elopement lets you have an incredibly special and intimate ceremony with just you and your spouse, an officiant, and a witness or two. (Along with a photographer of course, because I strongly believe those moments should be documented.) There is absolutely *nothing* wrong with having a larger wedding. Some of the best weddings I have been to had more than 100 guests! If this is what you want, seriously go for it! Packed dance floors are *always* a joyful sight at a wedding.

But again, if that guest list is something you really do not want to deal with, elopements are a great option. The average wedding in the US costs roughly $30,000—not including the honeymoon! If that number terrifies you, one thing that every single bride will tell you is that the easiest place to cut costs is *cutting the guest list.*

Let me tell you a secret: if you elope, you won't seriously hurt anyone's feelings. At least not anyone who truly matters.

If you decide to elope, it can save so much stress from wedding planning. In the end, it all comes down to what you and your future spouse want from your wedding day. Either way, there is no wrong choice, and the people who love you will keep loving you no matter how or where you and your spouse begin your wedded life.

ABOUT THOSE

GUESTS

You do not owe anyone an invite.

That's right. Read it again if you have to, over and over.

Please don't buy into the fact that someone can push his or her way around to get what they want on one of the only days in life where the focus is entirely on you and your loved one. When someone is upset about not being invited to your wedding, it's never a reflection of your decisions. It's a reflection of their sense of entitlement.

No one is owed an invitation. No one has a "right" to be invited. But also, remember that no one owes you anything. I'm obviously talking about a wedding, right? This does fit wedding situations, but it also applies to your entire life.

It's strange, the things that apply to both weddings and to life in general. No one is owed or guaranteed anything in life. We're not owed friends, or supporters, or invitations to anything. Sure, there will be people close to you who are more likely to support you and those whom you might want to be there and to witness your vows and celebration, but you're still not required to invite them or to include them in moments you feel are private or sacred *unless you decide to do so.* We are so lucky when we find people who truly support us because they love who we are. Look around in your life and see who those people are, who respect and love you for the person you've become. That includes honoring decisions and beliefs that you hold about your wedding day.

When it comes to *not* inviting people, I've probably heard every line in the book, from "My relatives would kill me" to "How can I not invite so-and-so?" but that still doesn't give anyone a free pass to your wedding. Dr. Seuss had it right when he said that those who mind don't matter and those who matter don't mind. Let's be clear, it may be a bummer. If I weren't invited to my sister's wedding because she chose to elope, I'd be sad to not share something like that with her, but ultimately it's her day. I can best support her by supporting what she desires for her wedding.

On the other hand, some couples want to invite a few people to be with them on their day. I get questions all the time from current and potential couples asking if they are "allowed" to have anyone else with them to witness their ceremony. The answer? Absolutely yes! An elopement doesn't mean running to the next town over and signing a marriage license alone in a courthouse. It can be you and a half-dozen of those

you love the most, together on a mountainside at sunrise. Whatever you have envisioned to be your "best day ever," elopement can be just that. Don't let anyone tell you that having guests present means it's not "a real elopement."

Since an elopement is anything you want it to be, so are the invitations. It can be something as simple as reaching out to those you love and letting them know they're invited to participate in your wedding day, or you can go all out and send personal invitations. You may want to consider special wording to emphasize that, though you are eloping, you are also requesting their presence at the ceremony.

"We've chosen to celebrate with an intimate ceremony with the people who have shaped our lives the most. Please join us if you are able."

"We're eloping! You're invited!"

"We've decided to elope and host a small ceremony surrounded by our closest family and friends. We would be honored if you joined us to celebrate our wedding day."

Those are just a few ideas to get you started and get your wheels turning. There's no right or wrong way to invite those you love to your elopement!

The next question that comes up is about who pays for your guests being there. This is completely up to you. If you're opting for a destination elopement, you do *not* have to pay for them to attend your wedding day. They can be responsible for their travel and lodging as well as booking it. However, if you are narrowing it down to just a small handful of people you want to celebrate with you and it's within your financial means to do so, of course, you can offer to cover any of their costs.

Most couples I've worked with do opt to pay for everyone's dinner after the ceremony, and the night before if there is a rehearsal, but again it's not necessary.

A kind gesture is compiling a list of local suggestions covering food, lodging, travel, and transportation that your guests can use while attending your elopement. I always work closely with all my couples to provide them with a goldmine of information regarding the area where they will be eloping. That way, they have it and can pass it along to anyone who may be joining them. Always feel free to reach out to your photographer (or other vendors) for recommendations if you need some, as they may have (because I know I have) plenty of resources for you to ease your mind and make your elopement as smooth as possible.

One thing I highly recommend is that you communicate clearly with your guests *before* your elopement to confirm their travel plans and make sure that they, and you, have contact information. You wouldn't want your best friend to get stranded at the airport because of a miscommunication. I've included a simple checklist below for basic information to gather from those who will be celebrating with you.

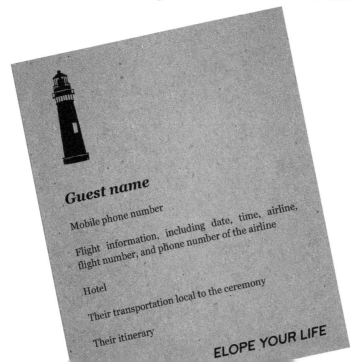

Guest name

Mobile phone number

Flight information, including date, time, airline, flight number, and phone number of the airline

Hotel

Their transportation local to the ceremony

Their itinerary

ELOPE YOUR LIFE

This leads us directly into our next question. What will my guests be doing the rest of the day after the ceremony?

I encourage all my couples to let their guests know that both before and after the ceremony they are welcome to go on their own adventures in the area, exploring local shops, restaurants, trails, and scenery. As I mentioned above, I strive to provide my couples with value, which means I go beyond just taking stunning photos of their wedding day. I also scout the area for the most unique locations to visit and see ahead of time and pass that along to you.

In my experience, as long as the guests know where they need to be and when, and you have a way of contacting them, every elopement and intimate wedding runs smoothly.

Communication is essential, which means you will also be responsible for letting your guests know if you will or won't be around before or after the ceremony. By explaining that you may be off on a hiking adventure for a few hours afterward to get some epic photographs, or stating that while you're getting your hair and makeup done before the ceremony you will be off-limits, you can avoid a lot of unnecessary stress and confusion about who is included in each activity during your wedding day.

Special considerations

If you choose to invite guests to your elopement, you will have to make a few special considerations for them, just like you would during a typical wedding planning process. Here are a few that I've run into and encourage my couples to think through before finalizing any decisions....

Location

You might dream of hiking to the top of a Colorado 14er, and you can't imagine your mother not standing beside you on your elopement day... but she suffers from extreme altitude sickness whenever she visits Denver. You may have to rethink a few things to make sure that you can be accommodating to those who are celebrating alongside you. Your grandfather may not be up for a three-mile hike before sunrise, and your best friend may not be able to afford a plane ticket to Ireland. So if you have your heart set on certain people being with you at your ceremony, you will need to take their needs into consideration as you choose your location (or how you organize your ceremony; for example, the three-mile hike may occur after the ceremony with just you, your spouse, and your photographer).

Who's invited

This goes for conventional weddings and destination weddings, intimate weddings, and elopements.... You don't have to invite everyone. Just because you invite one or two people from a family or friend group does not mean you need to invite them all. Are you close to your siblings but your partner hasn't talked to his or her siblings in a few years? It's 100 percent okay if your siblings are included but your partner's siblings are not.

You don't need to give anyone an explanation as to why you're choosing to elope or have an intimate wedding...or any decisions regarding your wedding day for that matter. However, keeping open lines of communication, a cool head, and a gracious heart goes a long way to ensure that relationships are kept intact during an emotional event like a wedding.

One final note on guests. Something I've noticed is that the closer someone is to you, the more he or she respects whatever decision you make, be that in life, love, or whatever. On the other hand, there are those (in all our lives) who, despite not being genuinely close, feel that they have a right to be included in whatever they deem valuable. That entitlement is a seed that takes root in one place but spreads to other areas of life. Entitlement doesn't limit itself to being invited to weddings. To take the metaphor a step further, don't water the bitter seeds. You are worth so much more than that.

THE

HARDEST PART

For a select few, the hardest part of eloping might be choosing a location, or telling friends and family, or even making the decision in the first place. In my opinion, the hardest part is not the actual decision. It's sticking to your choices, even if friends and family either don't understand or ask to be invited. When you are met with questions, and criticisms, and negativity... I get it. It's really hard to disappoint people. You could say that's the reason I didn't have an elopement and instead went through with a traditional wedding.

It's one thing to say that you are going to stick to your guns, but it's an entirely different thing to do it. Imagine someone looking at you with big puppy dog eyes and insisting that she will be invited to your wedding. Imagine someone asking you, "Why on Earth would you do something like that?" as if you were doing it to them. How would it possibly feel to have someone look you straight in the eye and then, with a tone of dismissal, say just one word, "*Why?*"

You might have friends and family say things like, "But you'll be disappointing so-and-so" or "Your sister was really looking forward to being your bridesmaid."

I won't even get into the fact that the latter sentence is littered with a ton of assumptions, including the sister expecting that she would automatically be a bridesmaid. People say things like that because on some level they want you to change your mind about what you're doing. They want you to choose what makes them feel good (and includes them). A lot of times the people who say these things don't even realize how powerful their words are.

We love our friends and family and we want to make them happy, but do we want to make them happy at the expense of our own happiness on one of the most important days of our lives? Eloping is still an unusual way to go about a wedding day, and people are bound to have questions and that's okay. Those questions are valid, but they should not under any circumstances make you feel like your wedding is inadequate or wrong just because you decided to elope on a mountaintop or travel to somewhere exotic and have an adventure, instead of standing in a church or banquet room in front of 200 people.

Your wedding day is worthy of whatever you want it to be, and you might have to keep telling yourself that. You and your partner should have each other's backs when it comes to reaffirming why you have chosen the wedding day that you both desire. A moment of making other people happy for something like a wedding is not worth the sadness and regret you might feel as a result. You need someone—who isn't your partner—to back you up and reaffirm your choices. Reach out to a trusted friend. Heck, reach out to internet groups of empowered elopers. Reach out to me if you want to. Just know that there are people in your corner to keep you feeling empowered about your wedding day.

I'M WORRIED ELOPING

WON'T FEEL SPECIAL

As an adventure elopement photographer, this is something I hear often when couples are debating whether to elope. And it makes me sad for a few different reasons. First, when a person says that, he or she is essentially declaring that it's the people who are invited to a wedding who validate a wedding day and make it special. Certainly, it is great when people are excited about your wedding, but the day itself is not more important than your own wishes. Arguably, your day is even more special because you are deciding that it's not about societal expectations or the pomp and circumstance of a traditional wedding.

Perhaps an elopement or wedding can be even more special because you are choosing to keep it intimate.

People are worried that when they elope, it won't feel special. So let's break down the main differences between a traditional wedding and an elopement. An elopement usually does not have a lot of guests. Every difference that I have seen between a traditional wedding and an elopement starts with the phenomenon of few or no guests. That includes no need for a big reception hall, cake cutting, wedding favors, bouquet toss, etc.

You are going to get dressed up (or stay casual, as you know I am a fan of *you doing you*). You will go to a place that is special to you, whether that is somewhere you have already been and want to return to, in order to create more memories, or to an entirely new place that you want to explore together. You're going to have an adventure. You're going to do things that represent you.

I encourage my couples to sit down and really think about the activities and moments that they love or want to experience. Is that a picnic? A hike? Is that backpacking to a chalet? Is it a hot air balloon ride? Riding horses? Gazing up at the stars on a blanket in the middle of the night? The possibilities are endless and the sky is quite literally the limit.

Do you love to kayak? Why not kayak in your wedding gear and be photographed doing something you are passionate about? Do you love to knit? Is origami your favorite thing? Would you and your future spouse love to re-enact funny moments in movies? All of these are possible and, at the end of the day, you are going to make a heartfelt commitment to the person whom you love.

So many people are afraid eloping won't feel special. But does special mean "witnessed" or does special mean "unique and intentional"? Only you can decide.

The guests, the cake, the reception, the first dance. It's all just extra stuff that we have decided, sometimes arbitrarily, constitutes tradition. All that stuff is secondary. It's secondary to creating a wedding day and a marriage and a life that represents the two of you. *That* is why your elopement day will be special.

WHY PEOPLE

CHOOSE TO ELOPE

People choose elopement for a wide range of reasons—and they might be very different from what you imagine. There are some common themes, yes, but everyone has distinct motivations for challenging tradition, being brave, and saying their vows the way they want to. I've polled newly engaged couples, past couples of mine, and anonymous contributors to discover some of the most common reasons people might want to elope.

They want a day that feels like who they are.

Not everyone is meant to have a huge wedding, complete with a wedding party, cake cutting, a reception, and the rest of it. Some people prefer the outdoors or keeping things simple. Society's expectations of having a big soirée can be wearisome for many people, and hosting a party that's devoted to all the attendees and not the couple getting married is not everyone's idea of fun.

The guest list (and other planning) is remarkably stressful.

I harp about Aunt Carol because that stereotype comes from somewhere. There's always a family member or friend who isn't necessarily close (but who knows, maybe they are close in your case) who has to have a say in everything wedding-related. The pressure to live up to expectations can be crushing. It's so much easier to start from scratch and plan everything without expectations in mind.

They want something genuine, intentional, and authentic.

This is not to say that a traditional wedding can't be authentic, but it's a lot harder with many outside voices offering their input. Your wants and needs can get lost amongst the din. As I mentioned before, a clean slate can get a couple back to the basics of who they are and what they want for their wedding and marriage. A traditional wedding comes with a lot of preconceived notions of what to include and what to exclude. It is hard to get out of that mindset, so tossing everything out and starting fresh can inspire a couple to think about every part of the day and whether it resonates with them.

They want to invest in things that are meaningful to them (a honeymoon, activities, photography, etc.)

There's a common theme that runs through what people tend to value: experiences rather than physical items. For some couples, spending money on things they won't have after the wedding day (plates, meals, favors, invitations) doesn't appeal to them. They desire lasting memories. They don't need more stuff to occupy their homes, but instead desire experiences and stories to share between themselves and with others.

They would love to avoid family drama.

I feel that everyone has at least a little family drama. Some people have dysfunctional families of varying degrees, and others have in-law issues. Whatever the drama or discord, some couples find it easier to circumvent those problems by avoiding a guest list altogether. Instead of worrying about family dynamics, the couple is free to focus on themselves and how they want to commence their marriage.

I would be remiss if I didn't mention cost. While yes, it is true that an elopement can be less expensive than a traditional wedding, that isn't the primary reason for choosing to elope. An elopement that has intention, intimacy, epic views and locations, a roughly structured day that represents the couple, and reliable and accomplished vendors won't necessarily cut a wedding budget from $20,000 to $2,000. In fact, one common reason to have an adventure elopement is that couples want those breathtaking images to remember their wedding day. *Eloping is a way to shift the financial focus from paying for guests to paying for things like location, the honeymoon, and photography.* It's more feasible to imagine a wedding budget going from $30,000 to $12,000 to $15,000 if a couple is set on a great location, honeymoon, photographer, and quality florals, attire, lodging, and travel. Again, this is all contingent on what the couple values most for their wedding day.

TRADITIONAL WEDDING COSTS
VS.
ELOPEMENT COSTS

Cost. Even with adventure elopements, it's not an insignificant factor. Lots of people weigh traditional wedding costs versus elopement costs as they are considering one or the other (or both). Some questions I have heard include:

"How much does it cost to elope?"

"Isn't eloping practically free?"

"How do you make a budget for eloping?"

Everyone has a budget, and your priorities dictate where you spend that budget. It's possible to elope and keep the costs to a bare minimum. Alternatively, you can still save money by foregoing a traditional wedding and choosing to create a fulfilling adventure instead. I preach that an adventure elopement is not a way to necessarily save 90 percent on wedding expenses, but it is a way to re-distribute your budget so that you spend the most on the things that are most important to you. It's about focusing on exactly how you want your day to look and feel—not what the wedding industry says it should look like, or how your family and friends say it should look. Let me repeat that last bit: *your wedding should not be based on how your family and friends think it should look.*

I firmly believe an elopement can be so much more than a way to save money or to get "pretty pictures." But still, it's helpful to understand the average cost of certain things, like the cost of an elopement. (Because is anyone made out of money? I know I'm not.)

I am going to tell you right now that the most significant expenditures of a traditional wedding are the venue and catering. For a guest count of 100 people, it adds up quickly. These numbers come from wedding professionals I know as well as national averages from WeddingWire.com.

Traditional Wedding Costs

Traditional wedding venue
$0 to $10,000 (the average cost in the US is $6,000)

Catering
$10 to $75 per plate; $45 per plate average, $27 average for a buffet ($45 x 100 guests = $4,500)

Décor and details
$500 to $800 ($700 average)

Photography
$3,000 to $10,000 (let's average this at $5,000)

Officiant
$250 to $450 (let's average this at $350)

Florals
$200 to $500 for a bouquet, boutonniere, and one smaller floral piece like a crown ($400 average)

Floral décor
$75 per table (12 tables, with 8 people each = $900)

Cake
Starts at $6 per serving (100 people x 6 = $600)

Wedding dress
$1,000

Hair and makeup
$300 is the average for a local artist

Total traditional wedding basic costs: $19,750

ELOPE YOUR LIFE

Elopement Costs

Elopement wedding venue
$0 to $500 (average cost for a permit is $100)

Catering
$0 (unless you'd like to treat your guests to a dinner at a restaurant)

Décor and details
$0

Photography
$5,000

Officiant
$350

Florals
$400

Floral décor (ceremony location, arch)
$500

Ten-night stay in an Airbnb (island of Maui)
$1,800

Plane tickets for 2 (New York City to Maui)
$1,300

Rental car (compact)
$575

Cake
$0

Wedding dress
$1,000

Hair and makeup
$300 is the average for a local artist

Total elopement basic costs: $11,325

ELOPE YOUR LIFE

Notes

It's not uncommon to see debates pop up on forums and threads, citing vendor directories. "But WeddingWire says that photography costs $2,000!" With that statement, there is an unspoken implication that photography costing more than that is "unreasonable" (one of my least favorite words). On WeddingWire and The Knot, I've found that with services like photographers, hair and makeup artists, etc., the average "booked price" is lower than the average actual price across the entire vendor spectrum, not limited to people who advertise on WeddingWire or The Knot. WeddingWire claims that the average cost of a photographer is around $2,000. It's important to know that their average is based on vendors booked through their site. This is partly because more people book lower-priced artists, and also because many higher-priced artists don't rely on WeddingWire as a listing source for their business. WeddingWire also fails to mention whether this is starting pricing (e.g., the low end of a range) or average booked price.

Based on my experience, and that of fellow photographers in the industry, average pricing for a full day of photography ranges from $3,500 to $6,000 for a traditional wedding or adventure elopement. I might make some enemies, but I'm going to be real with you, as always: the average couple who reaches out on WeddingWire or The Knot has a lower budget for vendor services. I personally don't think this is a good or bad thing. It is just what other wedding professionals and I have experienced. Of course, there are always outliers, hence the word "average." So, while WeddingWire and The Knot are full of vendors ready to make your day special, remember that their stats are not conclusive.

Did you notice how I included a honeymoon in the cost of an elopement? Many of my couples use their elopement destination and elopement ceremony as a kick-off to their honeymoon. They elope during the first part of their stay and have their first adventures as a married couple surrounded by their own version of paradise, cocooned in their own little world. Why did I choose Maui for this sample budget? Because it's a relatively faraway destination for most people, on the more expensive end to give a higher cost estimate (because better safe than sorry), and it's also still a domestic location for people in the United States.

PART THREE

LET'S DO THIS!

15

THE BASICS OF AN
ADVENTURE ELOPEMENT

Maybe you're at the point when you are thinking a non-traditional wedding is the way to go. But what in the world is an "adventure elopement?" In its simplest form, an elopement is the two of you and someone who has the authority to marry you. From my years in the field, I have learned that there are some must-haves for any adventure elopement.

The Experience

Above all else, think about the experience you want to have. Sure, it's made up of dresses, suits, officiants, photographers, locations, and the like. But more importantly, how do you want to *feel* on your wedding day? Excited? Relaxed? Calm? Like a goddess? Adventurous? Romantic? The list goes on, and there's no description that's off-limits for how you might want to feel. Once you've asked yourself that question, an important follow-up question is do you want to feel that amazing *only* on your wedding day or do you want to feel like that in other aspects of your life? Because ultimately, that's what *eloping your life* is all about.

An Officiant

The wedding celebrant can be religious or not. He or she can wax poetic if you want, or keep it short, sweet, and to the point. Being a licensed officiant myself, I tend to keep things simple when I'm photographing ceremonies in real-time. My advice? Getting an officiant you jibe with is essential for a great day. Some officiants have bubbly personalities, while others are more reserved. All will help craft a ceremony that reflects you, but naturally outgoing people will have an easier time with a fun, wise-cracking officiant. More reserved officiants will be able to effectively deliver a low-key, reflective experience.

Attire

We are going to stick with the basics and cover all the staples of attire. Remember: eloping is about running to what you truly love and who you genuinely are. Don't settle for attire just because you (or others) associate it with eloping if it doesn't resonate with you.

Let's begin with one of the most typical pieces of wedding attire: the dress. Ultimately, wear what you love. Unless it absolutely does not fit, you can't pick something that won't be stunning if you really connect with it. Part of wearing a stunning dress is the confidence and happiness that you radiate when you wear "the one."

There are some logistics to a more adventurous and outdoorsy type of elopement. It's not unfounded to be concerned about maneuverability. Make sure you're able to bend over, sit down, touch your toes, etc. A class 3 scramble up a mountain will be significantly more difficult in a form-fitting dress. Another thing to note, and most adventurous dress-wearers don't mind this, is that after spending some time outdoors your dress will probably have dirt on the bottom hem or the bottom few inches—usually not a ton, but it's something to be aware of if that's a concern.

Don't want to wear white? Don't! Plenty of spouses-to-be are opting for off-white, blush, grey tones and even black (I will be the first to say "Slay the day!" if you wear a black wedding dress).

The necessary footwear. I'm all for it if you want to rock a pair of Manolo Blahniks on your wedding day in the middle of the wilderness, though some logistics might cause you to adjust precisely how that dream comes to fruition. Overall, high heels don't go well with adventure weddings if you're wearing them for the entire day. Also, it's best to

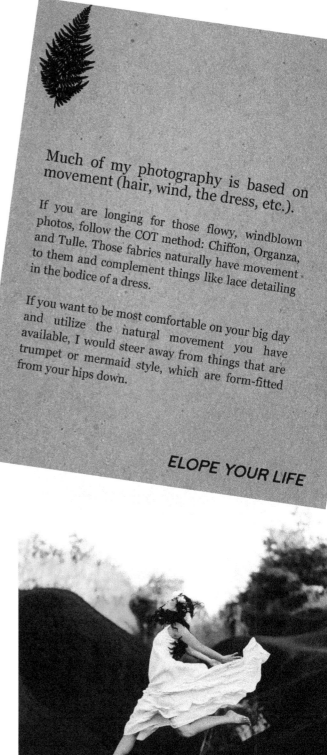

Much of my photography is based on movement (hair, wind, the dress, etc.).

If you are longing for those flowy, windblown photos, follow the COT method: Chiffon, Organza, and Tulle. Those fabrics naturally have movement to them and complement things like lace detailing in the bodice of a dress.

If you want to be most comfortable on your big day and utilize the natural movement you have available, I would steer away from things that are trumpet or mermaid style, which are form-fitted from your hips down.

ELOPE YOUR LIFE

avoid shoes with limited or no traction. They are a set-up for failure on wet logs, slick boulders, snow patches, and wet or muddy trails. There are plenty of options for cute and comfortable hiking boots. The vast majority of adventure elopement couples opt to forgo "dress shoes" entirely since they feel the boots add to the story (and I tend to agree). It's also a good idea to invest in a pair or two of some good wool socks. Wool stays warm even when it gets wet (you don't realize how grateful you are for warm socks until the ones you are wearing are wet and cold). I suggest getting some that are made by Darn Tough, Wigwam, or Smartwool brands—REI has lots of options. I personally really love Darn Tough and Wigwam, and Darn Tough even has a lifetime guarantee.

Suits, from snappy and jazzy to classic and timeless, tend to weather hikes well. If you have an outer layer (e.g., a suit jacket), this can easily be folded up and stored for any lengthy hikes. Detailing such as an interesting bow tie (bow ties are cool) adds dimension and a pop of fun with or without a suit jacket. To complete a suit look, a vest in a matching or complementary color works wonders and is another layer around your core in case the temperature drops a little.

If you get cold easily, heed my advice on this. For cold-weather wedding days, base layers are a must. For dress-wearing spouses, I recommend leggings, gloves, hats, etc. in nude or white (or the color of your dress). Blankets are also great, so feel free to bring a favorite along. Leggings or form-fitting thermal underwear work well under suit pants, too!

Don't ever feel like you have to subscribe to a stereotype or gender role in this. If you truly strive to make your attire unique, do your best to disregard the first idea or two that come to mind. Chances are they have been done many times before and possibly have been ingrained into your head as your first option. That is obviously not to say it's bad, but I bet there are better, more accurate ways to represent who *you* are when it comes to attire. From flowers to skulls to constellations to your favorite book characters—consider adding details to personalize even a basic piece of attire.

Location

There are lots of "adventure elopement photographers" who preach about hiking up a mountain and doing insane elevation gains like that's the only way to have an adventure. I look at adventure a bit differently. Sure, I'm up for backpacking through the wilderness to photograph you at a remote spot, but exploring the rugged coast of Oregon or hiking along Scotland's lochs and mountains are just as valid in terms of being *adventurous*. So is horseback riding on Kauai. I say, if it gets you active and outdoors (bonus points if it's something you haven't tried before), then I consider it "an adventure."

When thinking about a location, visualize what you are drawn to in terms of a backdrop. Some people love mountains, others want tropical beaches. Others prefer a more desert-like landscape. Once you narrow down the topography, think about whether you want to treat this elopement as the beginning of your honeymoon. Then consider whether you want to stay domestic or go international. From there, you'll have a good base

to work with when hammering out the finer details of exactly where you want to elope. A good elopement photographer knows multiple locations (domestic and international) that can fit with what you're yearning for.

Two easy questions and you've got a general idea of where you want to elope: backdrop, and domestic or international.

Who's Coming?

Last, but not least, the guests. This is possibly the biggest point of contention between couples. Perhaps you are thinking, "Aren't elopements meant to be without guests?" The definition of elopement is changing, I think for the better. So, back to guests. Do you invite family? Do you focus on yourselves and what will make you happy? There's no wrong answer except the answer that caters to everyone but yourself. You can have no guests present or you can have two dozen of your closest loved ones, as long as it's what you want.

I've had couples keep it a true secret. Other couples have invited some close friends and family. Some have invited no one but had a big party when they got back home after their honeymoon. There is no wrong way to do this, as long as you and your partner are happy with your decision.

16

TEN REASONS
ELOPEMENTS
ARE THE BEST

Not many people can say they took a helicopter ride or walked on a glacier on their wedding day.

Why conform to the typical white cake and garter toss when your day can be anything you and your partner desire? With an intimate wedding or elopement, you can incorporate personal touches and activities that make your day unique. That is one of the *many* reasons that elopements are so engaging. (Yes, that pun was intended!) Here are ten favorites.

1. You don't have to worry about guest-list-driven stress.

Guest lists are the basis of so much stress. Will your dream venue be big enough? Where will you house your guests? How will you feed them all? Should you provide alcohol? Do you have to invite your annoying cousins if you invite your aunts? All of these issues can be solved by cutting your guest list. As the wedding couple, you won't hear anyone say, "Well, a wedding reception is for free cake, food, and booze," but let me tell you, more people have that opinion than you might think. The more people who are involved, the more opinions there will be. Believe me. I've seen too many weddings where the guest list became a source of unending stress. *Everyone* has an opinion when it comes to weddings. And they will voice them. With elopements or more intimate weddings, you are free of so much of that drama. Your venue options open up. Do you want to elope to a mountaintop? You can do that much more easily with a handful of guests than with a hundred. You'll spend less money on feeding people, and your venues will most likely be less expensive. And guess what? You can still have a big party later!

2.   You can choose which ceremonial aspects to keep and which to "toss."

Elopements, by their very nature, go against convention. Do you want to wear an epic dress or have a gorgeous bouquet you can keep in a vase later? You can do that! Would you love to wear a dress that isn't white? Who's going to stop you? Elopements give you permission to make your day reflect what you value and enjoy.

3. It will be so much more intimate and relaxed than a formal wedding.

Small weddings and elopements typically lend themselves to being more intentional and genuine because they are not about pleasing everyone. With elopements (even when a few people are invited), the criterion has already been set: the celebration is all about you and your partner and experiencing the special moments of the day. You are already choosing an uncommon way of getting married, so you have the freedom

to design your wedding day as you envision it. That means that you will not be obligated to incorporate traditions that don't reflect *you* (for example, do you really want to toss that beautiful bouquet over your head?). Without guests and the intense pressure to make everyone happy, you can focus on having *fun* and enjoying the company of your spouse.

4. It's less expensive than a traditional wedding.

I'm not saying it will be cheap, but there are loads of benefits to this. With fewer guests, your catering costs will be almost nonexistent. Wedding favors? Forget 'em. A big venue to house your guests can be switched out for a $200 permit at a national park or beach. Side note: if you have a limited number of guests, it's free (no permit required) to elope on the Oregon Coast! Instead of trying to spread your budget over 50 list items, you can invest more into a dozen items and still not spend as much as you would for a traditional wedding.

5. You have more (and prettier) location options.

Finding a place that has the capacity for your guest list can be daunting. Will it fit everyone? Is it accessible to everyone? Is there room for a dance floor? Will the venue allow outside catering? When considering a venue, of the three principal qualities—space, attractiveness, and cost—you can choose only two. You can have space to house everyone in a gorgeous venue, but it'll cost you. Likewise, if you have a venue large enough at a decent price, it probably won't be very picturesque. With fewer guests, you can nix a lot of logistics, from dancing to catering, which opens up your venue options considerably. A good alternative for food is taking your few guests out to dinner, after eloping to an epic location like the coast or the Redwoods or a mountaintop.

6. Eloping is liberating.

As I mentioned before, the more people involved, the more opinions will be flying around. Everyone has an opinion when it comes to weddings. Plus, it feels better knowing that by not inviting anyone (except maybe a few people), you aren't singling anyone out. You won't be inviting a bunch of people but leaving out your second cousins whom you haven't seen in years and years yet they still feel entitled to attend your wedding. All of this means *you can do what you want* on your wedding day. And you don't realize how liberating that is until you actually experience it.

7. You've got a world of resources and recommendations at your fingertips.

The best adventure elopement photographers take on some aspects of the role of planner. They know the best florists, officiants, lodging, and permitting resources. They can also direct you to planners and coordinators who *specialize* in adventure elopements. Instead of taking recommendations from people who have hired only one makeup artist or florist, you've got recommendations from a photographer who has a great sample and you can choose the best for you.

8. Elopements take less time to plan.

Makes sense, right? Fewer things to coordinate means less time spent in front of the computer screen researching. I know so many couples who chose to wait a year or more before getting married because of the sheer number of things to pay for and organize. When you're eloping, you may still have things to plan, but it is a drop in the bucket compared to organizing tables, chairs, venues, guests, wedding parties, etc.

9. Big weddings are like funerals.

I'm not saying big weddings are sad. I'm just saying that, like funerals, they are mostly for the people who are invited. If you are fine with having your day focused on the guests, then go ahead and plan that big shindig!

But if you're more like me, and want the people at your wedding to be there for *you*, then consider cutting the guest list.

10. It's all up to you and your soon-to-be spouse.

Want to take a helicopter ride? Hike a few miles to a waterfall? The more people you invite, the more complicated incorporating something cool like that will be. Even if 50 or 100 people could fit near a waterfall to watch the ceremony, here's the likely scenario: you choose a waterfall location and invite everyone. Aunt Carol (she gets used as an example *a lot*) complains because she can't hike that far and feels like you're singling her out because of her inability to hike. *I have seen this happen*. But it doesn't have to be that way. Remember? *You do you.*

WOULD YOU

RATHER

People are conditioned to expect certain things when it comes to weddings. It's hard to break out of that mode. I know, I've been there. When you don't realize that extraordinary things are possible on a wedding day, it's hard to even dream them up in the first place.

The absence of guests loosens up the figurative corset that restricts wedding locations, logistics, and so many other things. Start thinking about your wedding day as if it were the biggest adventure of your lifetime, instead of a day centered around ceremony with guests, because, in reality, it really is the adventure of a lifetime. Marrying your partner is full of unknowns. But that's half the magic of the adventure—not knowing what's next. Your wedding day can be full of that same boldness.

When I ask couples what they would want to include on their wedding day, if logistics, budget, or any type of limitations were not a factor, often they aren't sure how to respond.

"I'd like photos of us in a cool place, and of the ceremony" is what they'll often say.

To me, that's a given. But you're eloping. You're bucking tradition by having a day you and your soon-to-be spouse design. So, what do you enjoy? Look at your partner and imagine a day with him or her. Envision having an adventure that you'll look back on and not want to change in the slightest. This is the time to think about the best memories you've created with each other so far. What did they include? Were you spending quiet moments together, seeing new sights, or laughing your heads off until you couldn't breathe? Think about the moments that reignited the spark that reminds you why you chose each other.

All that being said, what would you enjoy on your day?

When my couples are stumped by that question, I'll play a little game of "Would You Rather." This helps open their minds to activities, backdrops, and things that might have been on their "bucket list."

Would you rather SCUBA dive or ride in a hot air balloon?

Would you rather ride in a hot air balloon or a helicopter?

Would you want to do some hiking, or take a leisurely stroll?

Would you rather be too hot or too cold?

Would you prefer to do something you have already done, or to explore something new that you've always wanted to try?

Would you want to go somewhere new to create special memories, or return to a place that's already significant to you?

Would you rather make this an extended weekend trip or make this into a longer honeymoon?

Would you rather spend a day quietly reflecting, being bold and adventurous, or does it not matter as long as you're laughing and connecting with your partner?

ELOPE YOUR LIFE

Your initial answers to these questions may not be what you end up doing. They might not even be in the realm of how you ultimately choose to spend your day. You and your partner might not have the same responses. But that's okay. The important thing is that the questions get you thinking about elopement aspects that ignite something in your soul. Some of my couples want to get matching tattoos or hike overnight to a chalet in Glacier National Park for their wedding. Others want a simple picnic, or to go whale watching or on a wine tour. Whatever you do, let it be what you want to do, not something someone other than you or your partner has prescribed for you on your wedding day.

LET'S DO THIS!

Something else to keep in mind: you can still include things that you may find at a traditional wedding. Do you want flowers or a "first look" before walking down the aisle? Do you want an aisle? Do you want to have a reception at home after your trip? Just because you're not having a traditional wedding doesn't mean you have to completely discard every aspect of one.

Ultimately, the most important thing is to craft a wedding day that sets your soul on fire—whatever mix of traditional and nontraditional elements that means for you and your partner.

18

WHERE DO YOU WORSHIP?

I have found that you can feel deeply connected to a place, whether you have been there before or not. You may feel that a certain location calls to you and that you have always known you would someday go there. Do you have a place that calls to you? Is it someplace new? Someplace that reminds you of a spot you know? Someplace you are called back to time and time again?

I've never been an overtly religious person. My parents used to drag my sister and me to church almost every Sunday. It was a miserable experience for me. I never felt like I belonged, and the general group worship seemed like a cult to me. Don't get me wrong, please, because I do believe that religion can bring people together in a good way, too.

 In my opinion, the saying "I'm not religious, but I'm spiritual" has gotten a bad rap. Being spiritual can itself be sacred. One definition of religion is the worship of a higher being or higher power. The definition of worship is the feeling and expression of adoration. I don't feel that should be limited only to something as established as Christianity, Hinduism, or Islam. Why can't such adoration be of other beautiful things in life?

When I'm in the Coastal Redwoods of California, I feel like I'm experiencing another world. There have been many times I have gone to a lesser-known area of the vast expanse of the park to just sit and revel. I look up and think about how some of these titans have been alive since before Christ walked the Earth. There is a Native American story that says Spirit Beings were believed to be a divine race who existed before humans in the redwood region and who taught people the proper

way to live here. Eventually, they became the Redwoods themselves, continuing to guard over the forest. That is what I feel when I'm amongst them. I imagine all of my couples who have eloped in the Redwoods, who have had spirits standing sentinel over them as they said their vows.

I've done some of my best thinking among the Redwoods. I've experienced deep gratitude when close to these living, breathing giants. I've cried. I've smiled. And yes, I've prayed. To whom? I don't know, honestly. I just felt compelled to give thanks to whoever or whatever created such amazing things like redwoods, coastlines, mountains, and valleys.

I'm moved by nature. The existence of so many astounding things leaves me quite literally awestruck. I go to those special places to appreciate my surroundings, to be grateful in the moment, to remind myself to be grateful in other moments, and to reflect on the world we live in (for better or for worse). I was drenched in a mixture of tears and coastal rain one day in the Redwoods when I realized, *this is my church*.

Just like a church isn't any one building, and people relocate to different churches, I do the same. I feel drawn to certain churches more than others, but all have a message and can be a source of power and inspiration. My churches tend to be the titans of the Redwoods, the rugged Oregon Coast, or the peaks of the Crown of the Continent.

So, choose your church. That church can be made of brick and stone, or something less sturdy. Whether you get married in your church or not, make an effort to go back there to give thanks once in a while. I truly believe that the idea of a church is not limited to four walls.

19

AN ELOPEMENT IN
EIGHT STEPS

Some people (including me, sometimes) like an orderly list of what to do and when. For those people, here is how I recommend planning your amazing adventure.

The steps to planning an elopement or intimate wedding are a little different than planning a more traditional wedding. Instead of deciding on a venue as one of your first priorities, that can be done later in the process.

1. First, I recommend deciding what your wedding priorities are. People tend to choose from the following: location, photographer, videographer, attire, lodging, time away or vacation during your elopement, activities on your elopement day, selective guest attendance, décor, details, and more. Pick your top three to five priorities to which you want to devote most of your attention. You're going to invest, in terms of energy and finances, in these aspects. By that, I don't mean that you'll spend a majority of your budget on these things, but you should be spending the amount within your overall budget that will secure the location, vendors, and experience that you desire.

2. Once you have set your priorities, identify the locations that would work for your wedding day. Now, this isn't like choosing a venue. It's merely choosing a rough geographical and topographical area. Feel free to use the tips in the "Would You Rather" section of this book if you're having trouble narrowing down your choices. For instance, would you rather elope in the snow or someplace tropical? Would your preferred background be in the mountains, on the beach, or on the coast? Factors could include where you'd like to honeymoon immediately following or preceding your big day (yes, you can do that!), and whether you would like to experience someplace new or a place already significant to you.

3. Whether or not a photographer or a planner is high on your priority list, I want to share this with you: the best elopement photographers and planners are a treasure trove of information and they love helping their couples create a day that is fun, adventurous, one-of-a-kind, and connected. They will usually be able to give you insights related to the things most important to you, and locations that are perfect for your likes, dislikes, and interests. I've had couples come to me and say they prefer certain climates and have a distance range in which they would like to remain. From there, I help them learn about places that would fit their elopement day vision. A photographer or planner can eliminate so many steps between your ideal day and the people, like stylists and officiants, who can help make it happen.

4. Once you have narrowed down a rough idea of the location and a planner or photographer, stop and take some time to connect with each other. An amazing elopement day begins with preparing for it months before by connecting with your partner. You can have the most beautiful backdrop in the world, but if you're so busy rushing through the day or distracted and not in tune with each other, the backdrop won't matter. Take the time to plan a simple date night, or sit on the couch and talk about your ideas for the coming years. Ask questions. Be curious. There is always something more to learn about each other.

5. Work with your vendors to finalize items and tasks. You can choose to include or exclude anything you want on your day. Include or forgo flowers. Incorporate an activity like horseback riding, a guided tour, or whale watching. Or keep it simple with some easy sightseeing. Not only should you continue to connect with your partner, but also with the people who will be part of your day. I have found the best wedding days happen when couples stay in touch with the vendors who are most important to them. Check in with them on social media, send them a text message, or send them a hand-written card. It doesn't have to be wedding related. In fact, it shouldn't always be about the wedding day. Send photos of your wedding dress or shoe details, but also reach out just to say "hi." Getting to know the most important people who will be part of your wedding day is essential to everyone feeling comfortable and bonded. The best vendors will also want to reach out to you and get to know you on a level that makes you comfortable.

6. As the date nears, work with your planner or photographer to finalize a timeline, based on what you want to be captured on the day. But don't neglect to put as much importance into the time after the photographer leaves. Have a rough plan for your day

from start to finish. Your photographer may not be there to capture you two having drinks at sunset at a gorgeous viewpoint, but the moment deserves just as much thought and care. You'll still have things to look forward to long after the camera is gone.

7. **The day before your elopement**, take some time to soak it all in. So many couples are distracted with travel plans and making sure everything is in place that they neglect to slow down and enjoy the last day of their engagement with each other.

8. **Let your elopement day flow.** You have a schedule, but take what comes. It can rain or a road might be closed. While you do your best to avoid hiccups like that, no plan is foolproof, so enjoy the ride. Sometimes detours end up revealing something magical that could not have been planned.

There is a saying: tragedy plus time is comedy. I think of it as a reminder to take events as they come. Nothing by itself will derail or destroy your elopement day. Enjoy planning and logistics as they occur. Having the expectation that everything will go off without a hitch only sets you up for disappointment. Most of us know this, but sometimes it's good to be reminded.

Don't speed through everything in a rush to get to the destination. Revel and bask in the season of engagement, and take advantage of moments to bond with your partner and those who will be closest to you on the big day. Life is an adventure, and I've found that often, the best parts of an experience are the ones we don't plan for, but allow ourselves to celebrate.

20

HOW DO YOU
WANT TO FEEL?

Before we get into all of the possibilities for activities on your elopement day, it's important to consider something that is frequently overlooked. And that's unfortunate because your entire day is predicated on this question: how do you want to feel? What emotions and essences do you want your wedding day to evoke? You're certainly not going to jump out of an airplane if the word "adrenaline" doesn't once come to mind.

I encourage my couples to sit down and discuss how they want to feel on their big day. Many different words can be associated with an event as momentous as a wedding day. While some words are quick to come to mind, don't settle for easy-peasy "relaxed" or "stress-free." Let's do an exercise together. Consider the following list of words (and any additional words you feel inspired to add), one at a time. Think about images, feelings, sensations, and memories associated with each word. Close your eyes with me and imagine each of these words in turn. Create an image in your mind of what that word means to you. As an example, for me, the word "wild" means untamed. I envision nothing too perfect or polite. Hair whipping in the wind. No fine, perfect lines. Dirt. Mountains. Rugged beauty. Naturally beautiful. Green. Lupine flowers. Vines. Rocky terrain. Someone or something roaming the outdoors. Mustangs. Wolves. Freedom. Independence.

Visualize a setting that expresses the word completely. Do you have a memory associated with the word? Is there something you have always wanted to do that reflects the meaning of the word to you? I encourage you to write in this book! Circle the words that speak to you. Write down concepts and ideas that relate to your definition and vision of each word.

Wild

Adventure

Intimate

Free

Organic

Natural

Bohemian

Adrenaline

Excitement

Genuine

Urban

Strong

Independent

Unexpected

Remote

Untamed

Elemental

Seductive

Romantic

Earthy

Powerful

ELOPE YOUR LIFE

Bold

Uncharted

Homey

Comfortable

Rugged

Poetic

Artistic

Storybook

Intentional

Creative

Edgy

Free-spirited

Nontraditional

Exotic

Enriching

Educational

Engaging

Quirky

Laughter-filled

Heartful

Epic

ELOPE YOUR LIFE

Another way to consider how you want your elopement day to feel is to envision it. Imagine every detail. The backdrop, the dress, the suit, your hair, how your partner looks at you, the interactions between the two of you. From the overall image down to the minute details. Is your hair whipping in the wind? Are your lungs filling deeply with oxygen as you hike? Are you shouting for joy at the top of the world? Can you imagine feeling the earth beneath your feet? Picture the experience, and let words come to you to explain it. These words can include typical human emotions, but to have a better understanding of what your day should be, go past those words. Sometimes you might need to delve deep. Search for words like you're digging through a thesaurus. Not all the words listed above are emotions, yet nonetheless, they evoke *feelings*.

If you find yourself using other words on this list to describe an initial word (e.g., I used "freedom" to describe "wild"), that is okay! Words can be closely linked because of common ties. Continue to find other words, feelings, colors, and emotions to describe a word. Just refrain from thinking that because you've come up with "freedom" to describe the word "wild" that your job is done.

Write these words down. Choose your top three that you want to associate with your day. Keep them in mind when you consider locations, attire, florals, activities, and the overall vibe of the day. Put them in your planner as defining themes to constantly look back on. Write them on your bathroom mirror with lipstick. Put a sticky note on your computer screen. Whatever keeps those words close, do it.

Put together a Pinterest board (until it goes the way of MySpace, at least) with visuals that represent those words or a virtual or physical mood board of the same thing. Do a good, thorough collecting session. Then take a step back and look at the images you've gathered. If you haven't decided where to elope, or what to wear, or what to do, you may notice some common themes emerge from the images you've gathered—whether it's a common topography, color, activity, an exact location (e.g., lots of pictures of the Eiffel Tower), or type of location (e.g., mist coming in off the ocean at dawn). What stories are your images telling? And most important, how do those stories make you feel?

21

50 THINGS TO DO ON
YOUR ELOPEMENT DAY

Think of the best day ever. A day spent with your partner doing things you love, or trying something completely new. Here's the trick: don't think about this with a wedding day in mind. This day could have already happened, but I encourage you to go bigger and dream up something even better. Does the day include just the two of you? Does it include a few friends and family? Okay, now add on wedding finery and a commitment ceremony. Do you have it all in your head? Congratulations, you just came up with the beginnings of what your elopement wedding day could be.

Activity inspiration

Please don't rush through this list. Instead, think about each activity and whether it piques your interest. This is by no means an exhaustive list; it is only meant to get you thinking about possibilities.

ELOPE YOUR LIFE

1. Kayaking

2. Helicopter tour

3. Private boat tour

4. Sailing

5. Horseback riding

6. Dog sledding

7. Airplane tour

8. Hiking

9. Backpacking

10. ATV

11. Space nets

12. Dancing (simple or complex choreographed dance)

13. Wine or brewery tasting

14. Skiing

15. Snowboarding

16. Snowshoeing

17. Whale watching

18. Sandcastle building

19. Jumping into the ocean or a lake

20. Parasailing

21. Skydiving

22. Glacier sightseeing

23. Snorkeling

24. SCUBA diving

25. Visiting an animal sanctuary

LET'S DO THIS!

26. Safari

27. Surfing

28. Having a picnic together

29. Pub crawling

30. Tree planting

31. Hot air balloon ride

32. Sandboarding

33. Rock climbing

34. Bouldering

35. Fishing

36. Archery

37. Mountain biking

38. Motorcycle riding

39. Camping

40. Stargazing

41. Visiting hot springs

42. Volunteering

43. Roasting marshmallows around the campfire

44. Playing card games

45. Escaping from an escape room

46. Visiting a museum

47. Taking a Jeep tour

48. Ziplining

49. Witnessing an aurora borealis

50. Creating art (photography, painting, origami, etc.)

Do any of these call out to you? Perhaps they inspire you to create something that is 100% you and your partner. I know that I prefer outdoorsy ventures, but if you're happy waltzing into a movie theatre in your wedding attire and hitting up the latest Marvel movie, then I'm giving you permission right now to do it. Focus on the way you feel when you consider an activity. When you think of an idea and instantly have a positive visceral feeling about it, that's something to consider with your partner as a facet of your adventure wedding day.

22

SAMPLE ELOPEMENT
TIMELINE

An elopement planning timeline differs from a traditional wedding timeline. Typical timelines have tasks divided up by "months before the wedding." Couples come to me to help with eloping anywhere from one month to nearly a year and a half out. There is no set time to decide to elope. That said, I know that I still wish I had eloped a month before my wedding. And although this timeline works, it doesn't mean that you can't throw your big wedding plans away a month before the day. If elopement is for you, it doesn't have to take a year to plan.

What to Book First

Here are some things to consider regarding who books up first.

Even before you're engaged, you may know that a venue and photographer are two things you need to book right away when planning a wedding. I mean, couples planning a traditional wedding look at venues and check their booked dates before a ring is even in the picture. With planning an elopement, it's a little different.

You can still use lots of the same wedding vendors (like a photographer, makeup artist, floral designer, etc.) when planning an elopement, but the order in which you book is different. Let me explain. You don't have a typical wedding venue. This is the big thing that shakes up the order of stuff. Most couples start in one of two states of mind:

1. You already know your location and you do your own research figuring out what permits are needed, if any. Let's say you have been to the Redwoods and *know* that is where you're getting married. That's a major decision narrowed down. Then find a photographer with whom you'll get along and who knows a lot about the Redwoods (*ahem*). Important note: If you are *really* digging on a particular photographer but aren't set on your date or location, choose your photographer first. Then work out the logistics for the days she or he is available.

2. You're not sure about your location. Maybe you could celebrate your wedding in Glacier National Park, but the Oregon Coast excites you, too. That's where a photographer who specializes in small weddings and elopements comes in. This is a "two birds, one stone" sort of thing. Elopement photographers usually know their stuff when it comes to lots of different locations. Book your photographer who is an expert on locations first, then decide together what the best place is for your ceremony.

The cool thing about hiring an elopement photographer...

...is that a lot of us specialize in knowing all about those locations that you may have been dreaming of. I ask my clients questions about their likes, dislikes, and really get to know them so that I can recommend locations that will speak to them and best represent them. Planning an elopement does not have to be a nightmare, and with an adventure photographer to help, it will be, dare I say, *fun*.

And now for a timeline.

Initial Planning Tasks (anywhere from 5 to 12 months out)

Narrow down a rough idea of a backdrop you might want for your elopement. It doesn't have to be specific, but a general idea, such as "mountains" or "ocean" helps a lot.

Find a planner, photographer (and possibly) a videographer you like. They tend to book far in advance, and will likely also have ideas on locations. An elopement photographer who serves couples well will have advice that is beneficial regardless of whether you've chosen a specific location or still need help narrowing that down. Take note, not all photographers are created equal in this respect. Find one who fits your expectations and price point. A good rule of thumb (though not always entirely accurate) is the adage, you get what you pay for. Some photographers provide more planning assistance than others. There are those who have a different editing style. There are countless different approaches a photographer could have regarding his or her craft. Some may require a phone consultation to ensure that you are a great fit for each other. You might be able to book others from email communication alone. Some prefer to be a fly on the wall during your elopement, while others are more like that "cool friend" who is always down for laughs and adventure. Ultimately, the experience you have with a photographer is just as important as price point, and shouldn't be overlooked.

Select wedding attire if it requires time to finalize. A tailored tux, and especially a traditional wedding dress, can require months for alterations.

Intermediate Planning Tasks (4 to 10 months out)

Finalize your location.

Book your photographer.

Begin learning about and meeting with vendors you are interested in, like florists, hair and makeup stylists, officiants, and local guides. I recommend prioritizing vendors who are able to serve only one couple per wedding day, like hair and makeup artists, and officiants.

Put a rough plan together of how you will be getting to the place where you will elope and where you will be staying.

Book your lodging.

Final Planning Tasks (1 to 2 months out)

Roughly four to six weeks out, many photographers and planners will help you put together a timeline for the day.

Book any travel you need (flights, rental cars, etc.). Tickets are typically at their best price about six weeks out from the date of travel, depending on whether you're traveling internationally or domestically.

Finalize and pick up wedding attire.

Submit wedding permits if your location requires them.

Confirm where and when you will need to pick up your marriage license. Some states and countries have waiting periods, or their city hall, register, or county clerk may be far from your elopement location.

Your timeline may look a little different than the one above, and that's okay. This is meant as a guide, using plans, vendors, and items that many couples might want to incorporate. When in doubt, always try to get things finalized as far in advance as possible.

Lodging

Whether or not you are inviting guests, lodging is the next thing to take care of after booking your photographer and deciding your location. Places surrounding locales like national parks often book up to a year in advance.

Smaller (but still important) details

I provide an elopement guide to help you choose the perfect outfit. If you're wearing a dress, I help you select a dress based on fabric to allow movement for images, and also something that fits your body type. You can incorporate anything you would like into your elopement day—from florals to a hot air balloon ride, horseback adventure, or an epic hike leading to a majestic view. We will work together on brainstorming those pieces so that your day is fun-filled, but leaves room to relax and not feel rushed.

23

ELEMENTS OF AN
ELOPEMENT DAY

While many parts of an elopement day resemble a traditional wedding, there are key differences that are possible because of having few or no guests. Traditional moments like getting ready, the ceremony, and portraits have a place with elopements, and what's more, there are often twists to make them personal. Without guests, there are other moments that can be incorporated, too.

Getting Ready

When planning your elopement, I encourage you to consider details you might not have thought about yet. Do you desire a ceremony at sunset so you can wake up at your leisure, and have plenty of time to get ready together? Do you want a stunning sunrise ceremony that almost guarantees fewer

people at the location, and you can have the rest of the day for your first adventures as a married couple?

Do you want to get ready together, or separately? Are you longing for some photos of you slipping into your gorgeous wedding attire? Is getting ready going to be low-key enough that you would enjoy sleeping in a tent the night before, or would you prefer a cute cabin, yurt, or Airbnb?

The time when you are getting ready sets the tone for the entire day, yet many couples rush through this part in order to get to everything else. Don't neglect to nourish those moments when you can't help but stare at your fiancé(e) because you are just so thrilled at the prospect of spending your life with your beloved. Think about the smile on your face as you help each other get ready. Do you often tease each other? Make jokes? Love to annoy the other person (although they secretly love it and you know it!)? These moments are the ones that we want to remember—and we don't often realize it until they're gone.

The Ceremony

Your ceremony is truly the most important part of the day. Even if it's going to be "super short and low key," it is a special moment and I recommend doing it justice. That could mean slowing down, reflecting, and having music play on a portable Bluetooth speaker. I am a huge advocate of writing your own vows to read each other. My husband and I wrote our own vows, which incorporated our own brand of humor and inside jokes and allowed us to include things that were special to us.

I would be rich if I had a nickel for every time someone mentioned that he or she wrote their vows the night before the wedding. In some cases, couples have written them on the car ride to their ceremony, or not even written them at all. That is just doing a disservice to the official ceremony. I am a firm believer that your entire elopement day can feel like a ceremony and celebration, but there will always be that moment where you stand, facing each other, and recite your vows to seal the deal.

Having an experienced officiant can bring a whole new magic to your ceremony. While some vendors (like myself) are licensed officiants for those really casual and remote moments, it is simply not the same as having someone dedicated to guiding you through the ceremony and commitment process.

During my wedding to Brian, the part I really loved was the ceremony. There are times when I kick myself for not already having quotes from our ceremony framed on our walls. It was completely "us." We chose someone who knew us both, and she insisted on making the ceremony a complete surprise. The words she chose were whimsical, fun, intentional, and perfect. That intimacy can happen whether your officiant has known you for a long time or not. A good officiant will take time to get to know you personally, and dive deep beyond the surface of your relationship.

LET'S DO THIS!

I would like to share portions of our ceremony to show you that you don't have to stick to "I Do" (or, really, anything that is typical of a ceremony). Brian and I love things like *Doctor Who*, *Alice in Wonderland*, and *The Princess Bride*. So that's what we incorporated:

> *Welcome! It is my privilege to officiate this wedding of Brian Simshauser and Samantha Starns, both of whom I've known for many years now, having met them individually through participation in local theatre and music. They have invited us to participate in an important moment in their lives—one that will be profound, and intimate, and—curiouser and curiouser—as you will come to understand.*

> *Of course, unless I'm wrong, and I'm never wrong, you will encounter difficult times. Someone once said, 'Life is pain. Anyone who says differently is selling something.' Well, that's silly. There is so much more—life is triumph, and laughter, and exquisite delight....*

Brian wrote his vows.

> *I, Brian, take you, Samantha, to be my lawfully wedded wife. I do this today in front of our friends and family not because your father is holding the shotgun, but because I wake up each morning and make the choice to love you. Because we share adventures. Because I can't bear the thought of what you would do to Leo if I weren't around. I love you more than Otter Pops, but please don't make me prove it. Today I make my vows to you. I promise to love, honor and cherish you, in sickness and in health. Unless the sickness is a zombie apocalypse, in which case, I reserve the right to enact the "death do us part" clause.*

> *In the words of Dr. Seuss that I made up:*
> *I will love you if we're poor*
> *I will love you if you snore*
> *You I will keep to have and to hold*
> *Until such time that stars go cold*
> *I ask you love me all the time*
> *Even if my words don't rhyme*
> *I will love with all my heart*
> *I will love 'til death do us part*

And here are my vows.

Brian, you're my best friend. You know me better than anyone else in the world, even better than I know myself sometimes. You see the good, the bad, the hangry, everything—and yet you've chosen to travel through life with me. I'm constantly in awe of your compassion and humor and consider myself lucky every day that you make me laugh, or in many instances, roll my eyes. In return, I will do the best I can to be deserving of you.

I promise to split the money I find in your laundry with you 50/50. I promise to not start a Game of Thrones episode until you're comfortably seated on the couch and to always enlist your help in building outrageous geocaches. I vow to never stop falling in love with you. I promise to be your shoulder to cry on, the person who laughs at your jokes (most of the time), and to be your faithful companion through time and space. I have seen the best of you, and the worst of you, and I choose both.

And our "I Dos"? Instead of saying just that, our officiant chose different words for us to say.

Brian, wear this ring always.

Let it remind you that I have chosen to love you for the rest of my life,

And that I will choose again each day to love you,

and to let laughter strengthen our bond and ease our troubles.

Brian then responded, *As you wish.*

The moment I realized I would also be saying "As you wish," I started crying. Because it just felt right. If you know *The Princess Bride*, this quote is familiar to you. Even if you haven't seen *The Princess Bride*, chances are that you still are familiar with the quote and know that it comes from a well-loved movie. Somehow, our officiant, Kim, knew that "I Do" wasn't our style, without us ever saying a word about it.

LET'S DO THIS!

Your ceremony should represent *you*. If you are more introspective and quiet, or quirky and nerdy, it doesn't matter. A ceremony can be designed to reflect the relationship and commitment that you are making that day. It does not need to be trendy or have the perfect arch as a backdrop. It just needs to be intentional, honest, reflective, and representative of the life you want to build and continue to lead together.

Even if you are writing your own vows and keeping it simple, I highly recommend putting some thought into them and not writing them out on the car ride to your ceremony, or the night before. That leads to anxiety and panic, which are generally not feelings you want to associate with vows.

Another thing to consider is your religiosity. Do you subscribe to some type of spirituality? Symbolism ranges in ceremonies from devout Christianity to a celebration of the four elements.

Things people incorporate into their ceremonies....

Handfasting

Readings

Blessings

Popping champagne

Ring warmings

Prayers

Involving talents
(guests or the couple)

Tasting of the four elements of food

Surprise gifts

Surprise guests

Meditation

Moments of silence

Pets

ELOPE YOUR LIFE

The Officiant

Oh yeah! That person, the one who actually makes things official. A good officiant is often overlooked because he or she "just says a few words," but when it comes to adventure weddings, a good officiant is extremely important.

The best officiants for adventurous weddings love adventure and want to customize your ceremony to fit you and your partner's personalities. Great adventure officiants are comfortable outdoors and are not deterred by adverse weather. They also need to be versed in the state and location where you are getting married. Each state (and sometimes county) has different requirements for officiants in order for things to be legal and on the up and up.

Some couples just want something simple—no pomp and circumstance. They just want to devote their lives to each other with some simple vows or letters and let it be done. And that's a perfect opportunity to make sure your vows are strong.

Portraits

This part is probably what you see most when you look at images from an adventure elopement day. Depending on how you want the day to go, you can spend anywhere from a few hours to all day (or overnight) photographing. In between, there is hiking around, exploring new places, hanging out, changing locations, and of course, your ceremony.

Different photographers have different shooting styles. Some have a very posed method, while others are purely documentary and don't direct you at all. Still, there are others (like myself) whose style reflects a mix of posed and documentary, getting the best of both worlds.

In terms of photographs and the location, couples explore either a few places that require longer to get to or more places that are all easily accessible. Regardless, you and your photographer should work together to pick the perfect spots for you. For hiking, gauge up to one mile per hour of photography booked (a two-hour collection = up to two miles of hiking). That allows for time to hike, stop for breaks, photos, etc.

Try to keep hiking in your wedding dress to one or two (easy) miles at most. Less than a mile is ideal. I encourage my couples to wear footwear that is comfortable, fun, attractive, and reflective of their day. And if you desire a longer hike, a great pair of hiking boots worn with your wedding attire checks all those boxes.

Activities

Depending on your location, there are lots of different options for how to spend the day. Start off by thinking about what your hobbies are. Do you like to kayak? If you're eloping in an area where there's a lake or other safe body of water, why not kayak? Why not ride horses if that's your passion? You are already throwing those typical wedding traditions out the window. Start from the beginning and invent a highly intentional day full of the things you love.

ELOPE YOUR LIFE

Couples can enjoy (and have enjoyed):

An epic picnic

A first dance to your favorite song

A hike to a waterfall

A boat or kayak ride

A hot air balloon or a helicopter ride

A new hobby, like geocaching

Going on an interpretive tour

Backpacking to tent camp or staying in a chalet

Snorkeling

Getting matching tattoos

Starting a new tradition

Going on a guided horseback ride or whale watching tour

Including or basing your ceremony around an activity you both enjoy

Keep in mind that these are merely suggestions and if you want to go in a different direction, do it! Try something new or break out a special hobby. As long as it is significant to you, it is a great wedding day activity.

Some of the best and most personal elopements I have witnessed incorporate a mixture of typical intimate moments, like getting ready, and unique hobbies and activities that the couple loves to do or wants to try. This doesn't mean that you have to go all out for your day. Some of the times I've found myself tearing up the most have been during intimate, but super meaningful ceremonies that don't include anything "epic" aside from the love and connection the couple shares.

24

HOW TO TELL
FRIENDS AND FAMILY
YOU'RE ELOPING

When I got married, I didn't even know how to talk to people who weren't invited to the wedding, and I certainly didn't think about how to tell friends and family we wanted to elope.

I'll be the first to admit, wedding planning can be overwhelming (*I know*, I went through it). The expectations of tons of people are weighing on your shoulders. There's the looming guest list, a mother-in-law who just decided she wants an off-white dress and for you to invite a list of people you don't know. And don't even get me started on how creating a seating chart is the single most political thing you will ever do until you decide to run for office one day.

It kind of makes you want to throw caution to the wind and say "What the heck! *Let's elope!*"

The first thing you need to decide is if you're going to tell friends and family that you are eloping. Maybe your idea of an elopement is just the two of you exchanging

vows on a mountain or a beach. Perhaps you'd prefer a more intimate setting with your parents or a few witnesses. There's no "right way" to elope but there are pros and cons to telling people.

Before you go any further, know this:

The decision for you to elope and to tell people should *not* be taken as a Q&A or a request for permission from those closest to you. Because it isn't a request. It is a courteous acknowledgment that you've decided to follow your beliefs and desires instead of conforming to a traditional event that isn't your style.

PROS: People will get to feel like they're part of an inner circle, like your own secret elopement club. They'll feel pretty special because you decided to tell them, plus clubs are great. The people whom you do choose to tell often are people who are very close to you and have your best interests at heart, so they will likely be supportive and encouraging.

CONS: This is important if you truly want to keep things secret. So you told just that *one* person at work (or even a family member or close friend)? Well, they let it slip to another person at the office that you're eloping. The likelihood of the word getting out obviously increases as you tell people. Loose lips sink ships. (Loose lips ruin surprise elopements...? *Just doesn't have that same ring to it.*) The more people who know, the more opinionated people will get (*trust me on this one*). They'll start getting pushy and ask to be invited (or have "thoughts" on why you are "getting married like that"). If you decide to go this route, make sure you highlight the fact that it is a *small and intimate* ceremony, and it's what you and your fiancé or fiancée want.

My personal advice? If you want to tell someone, consider telling only your closest two or three friends or family members. Even then, be judicious about it, and emphasize until you are blue in the face that it's supposed to be kept on the down-low. For me? I know *right off the bat* that my dad can't keep his mouth shut so I would have a better chance of telling my mom or a close friend and keeping it quiet. I love my father, but it's the reality of the situation.

Worried about how to broach the subject? Try this:

"Mom and dad, we wanted to let you know that my fiancé(e) and I have decided to have a more intimate and private destination wedding, an elopement. After a lot of discussion, it is really what is best for us and what represents our personalities and our partnership. Even though we are choosing to go this route, you are special to us and will be in our thoughts and hearts."

See how there was no room for discussion or questioning? At that point, many people start to understand. If they still object, know that's a reflection of *their* character, not yours.

Do you want to include your family without actually having them there for your ceremony? Ask them if they would help with other events, like a wedding shower.

Have a "send-off" party a few weeks or even shortly before you depart for your elopement! This can be a chill event at a bowling alley, or as big as a typical reception. My advice: If they really want it, they need to help plan it in some way. Ask them to write a letter of marriage advice or a letter of love for you and your partner to read during your ceremony.

If they are only slightly bummed (it is better if they are totally okay with it, since this next option can be seen as adding insult to injury), have them help choose your destination if you haven't officially decided yet.

Give them choices, like "We've narrowed our destination down to X, Y, and Z, and we'd love it if you helped choose!" Invite a close friend or family member to go with you to pick out a dress or suit.

Not up for telling your family and friends beforehand? I've seen elopements announced in every way you can imagine. I have even seen couples surprise their parents by FaceTiming them from the ceremony. By far the most popular seems to be a mailed announcement.

My personal favorite wording is something I saw on an elopement announcement sent to me by a former couple (and current friends!):

Jack and Jill exchanged vows in a private ceremony at _____.

Although we decided to celebrate our love with just each other, please know that you were in our thoughts and will be forever in our hearts.

We couldn't be happier!

25

ELOPEMENT ANNOUNCEMENTS

Like "Jack and Jill" in the previous chapter, you might be thinking about sending elopement announcements. Sometimes you need a little help crafting the perfect announcement, so here are a few examples. This will also give you the opportunity to convey how important your friends and family are, even if they were not present for your ceremony.

We eloped!

On January 1, 2021, we said our vows in an intimate ceremony that best represented us and the life we wish to cultivate together. Though we chose to have a private ceremony, please know that you were in our thoughts and hearts. We couldn't be happier!

Jack and Jill eloped!

January 1, 2025

California Redwoods

In reflection of the couple and their interests and passions, an intimate ceremony was held with just the couple in attendance. Please join in congratulating them on this new chapter of life together!

§

We're Married!

September 3, 2021

If you know us, you know that we don't do anything typical. We decided to have an intimate ceremony in a place that we both love and feel reflects us as a couple. We are so lucky to have such amazing loved ones in our lives and are sending our love and thanks, for helping us become the best versions of ourselves.

§

Let this raven serve as notice that:

Jon of House Stark and Sabrina of House Targaryen

Have eloped on the island of Dragonstone (Maui)

February 14, 2022

The couple chose to commit their lives to one another in a private ceremony surrounded by the natural elements of ice and fire (Haleakala volcano). The privacy of their union was of utmost importance, though their friends and family (Houses Stark, Targaryen and beyond) continue to hold the highest place of honor in their hearts.

LET'S DO THIS!

We Eloped!

But We Love You and Still Want to Party

Please join us in celebrating our recent elopement by attending our party reception at _____, on May 4, 2025. First drink is on us!

§

Erika has stage fright

Justin hates crowds

So they eloped!

Erika and Justin chose to commit themselves to one another in an intimate ceremony with only immediate family in attendance on the Isle of Skye. Let us lift our glasses to congratulate the new couple on their meaningful ceremony and their new life together!

26

FIVE THINGS TO KNOW
WHEN ELOPING IN
A NATIONAL PARK

Over the past few years, there has definitely been an increase in people who choose to get married in grand and beautiful locations. Naturally, people are drawn to national parks, and when you think about it, it makes perfect sense. National parks are the best of the best, and the national park system chooses the best of the best to regulate and commercialize to some level. Of course, there are other amazing little-known locations, although those often don't have the vast expanse or infrastructure that national parks have.

Epic views of national parks come with a lot of tourist aspects that people should know about. If you're a visitor, these pieces of information are important. But they are even more crucial when you decide to elope in a national park.

Here are what I consider five of the most important things to know if you want to elope in a national park....

1. To elope in a national park, you need a permit.

First of all, no matter what national park you choose for your elopement, you are going to need a permit that comes from a special permit office and special event office within that particular park. In most instances, you can submit your application via email, but sometimes the park requires you to send them via post. These permits range in cost from $100 to $400 or more. The turnaround time for these really varies. I have seen parks require securing the permit a minimum of two weeks before the big day, while I have also seen parks, like Crater Lake National Park, require at least a six-week turnaround time.

2. Ceremony locations may be limited.

In order to prevent degradation of the environment and topography, the park will often tell you when you apply for a permit that only certain areas are allowed for ceremonies. This is especially true in parks like Rocky Mountain National Park where the prevalence of intimate weddings has led to limits on ceremonies and yes, even vow renewals, to roughly two locations. You might be dreaming of that beautiful view in Glacier National Park up at Logan Pass, but I am sorry to report that due to crowds, ceremonies are not allowed there, either. The same is true for some pristine locations that you may have seen in places like the Redwoods.

3. Consider the crowds.

Because the National Park Service made these amazing locations so relatively accessible, it stands to reason that people would want to visit them. Most people who are having traditional weddings do so on Fridays, Saturdays, and Sundays. This is when guests typically are off work and most likely available. If you think about it, those days are also prime opportunities for visiting parks.

As a result, to avoid the brunt of the crowds at national parks, it's best to have a ceremony on a Monday, Tuesday, Wednesday, or Thursday. Now that's not to say that those days won't be crowded at all, but they will likely be less crowded than Fridays through Sundays.

Crowds are also huge during the holidays. Keep that in mind when you are thinking about a long weekend such as Memorial Day, 4th of July, or Labor Day.

4. Your elopement location is beautiful, but is it special?

Now, I am going to call out a specific park because it is arguably the biggest offender. I went to Yosemite National Park on a Monday in October, which is the off-season or "shoulder season" (a time between peak and off-peak seasons). I pulled up to Taft Point to photograph a couple and on our way to the point and during the hike back, we saw no less than three other couples in fancy wedding attire with their photographers and entourages in tow. I don't know about you, but to me, an Instagram-famous location starts to feel a lot less special when more than one ceremony is going on at the same time.

I urge my couples to consider why they are eloping in a place if it's really popular. If it means something to you, then great. But if you are just going there because it's Instagram famous (and I strongly encourage you to think about whether that's a motivator), maybe we can find another place in the park or another park that has similar views that you can discover together as a new location.

5. The time of year matters.

I've lost count of the couples who have contacted me to elope at Crater Lake National Park and who want to get married there in January or February, but still want classic views of the lake. Crater Lake is covered by snow for at least six months of the year. Most of Rim Drive is not even accessible from mid-October through May. In the winter, the lake is obscured almost 80 percent of the time. The weather creates a trap in the caldera. Fog, mist, and clouds often get sucked into it.

If you want to elope at Crater Lake in the winter, then awesome! You just need to be prepared for the weather. The same goes for a lot of other locations, including Rocky Mountain National Park, Glacier National Park, and the Grand Tetons. Any place that isn't close to the equator may have adverse weather, which means anything from torrential downpours in the Pacific Northwest to scorching heat in the desert.

There you have it. My top things to consider when eloping in a national park. These are just a few of the things I discuss with my couples to make sure that they have a clear vision of what they want their elopement day to be like.

27

WHEN NOT

TO ELOPE

Some of the main reasons people elope are because they want to get away from expectations and all the stuff that comes with them. They just want to be in their own little world and celebrate on their day.

That means avoiding being in an overcrowded area. Some days of the year and week make that difficult. Because if you're eloping to a gorgeous place, there are going to be days that are busier than others. And I can't be the only one who doesn't like the idea of throngs of people nudging past you when you're trying to say your vows (*yikes*).

You are already bucking tradition by eloping, so this is your little reminder that you are not attached to specific days and times of the year. Ultimately, you are not attached to anything that comes with a traditional wedding (like when guests can and cannot make it).

Some people are attached to a specific date, like 10/10/2020 or 2/22/2022. It's all about your priorities—whether you feel the date or the lack of crowds is more important. If your priority is a lack of crowds, then "When do I *not* want to elope?" is a pretty important question.

If there is one day of the week on which you should not elope, it's a Saturday. That seems counterintuitive given that so many weddings take place on Saturdays. But here's the thing: if you're going to the Redwoods, or going to the Oregon Coast, somewhere on Kauai, Glacier National Park, weekends, *particularly Saturdays*, are going to be insane.

And it's not just Saturdays, it's really weekends in general that cause crowding for adventure elopements. I strongly recommend staying away from Saturdays and Sundays if at all possible. The next highest offender is Friday because people get off work early or take long weekends. Ultimately, I advise against Fridays through Sundays if you want to keep the traffic flow of the public to a minimum.

Don't forget the holidays. I know it's tempting to schedule an exciting trip when you can get time off because of a holiday. But any national holidays, any time when people are off work, they are going to want to go outside. Especially in the shoulder seasons and in the high season like May, June, July, and August for the northern hemisphere. While that's arguably when you will experience the best weather, depending on where you go, the shoulder seasons can be just as gorgeous! Search the off-seasons for specific places. Hawaii's off-season is actually the shoulder season for the northern hemisphere. It's still beautiful there, but far less busy.

One of the reasons for choosing to elope is to avoid all the hassles of planning. By booking an adventure elopement photographer who has location knowledge, or is known for extensive research on locations, you'll have help finding those little-known locations that aren't on the "most-traveled" tourist lists.

28

MARRIAGE LICENSE

BASICS

Marriage license requirements differ from state to state in the U.S., but in general, there are some things to consider to obtain a marriage license in the county and state where you will be holding your marriage ceremony. You go to a county clerk's office at a local (to your ceremony) courthouse to obtain your license (some counties let you apply online, but you will likely still have to pick it up). You will need to bring at least some form of ID, if not photo identification. My advice? Be safe. Bring photo ID and possibly a backup form of ID. Many places have a waiting period of a couple of days, though some are able to waive this, and some counties don't have a waiting period at all. You need to return the official paperwork to the county clerk. There is typically a $50 to $85 application fee, depending on the state.

Marriage licenses do expire (usually 10, 30, 60, or 90 days after issuance). Most states no longer require blood tests (check with the state where you will be getting married). Some states do not require witnesses, though I always feel they are a nice addition if possible.

Here are a few tidbits from all 50 states. Be sure to check your county clerk's website for specific information and any new updates.

Alabama

Beginning in 2019, Alabama courts no longer issued marriage licenses. Instead, couples submit notarized forms to probate judges. The marriage becomes legal once the probate court records the completed form. Please visit the Alabama Public Health website for more information and to obtain a certificate.

Alaska

Alaska requires two witnesses at the ceremony. There is a three-day waiting period, and the marriage license expires after three months.

Arizona

There is no waiting period in Arizona. Two witnesses of the signing of the license are required and the marriage license is valid for one year.

Arkansas

In Arkansas, there is no waiting period for people over 18 years of age; for those under 18, there is a five-day waiting period. Witnesses are not required, and the marriage license is valid for 60 days.

California

There is no waiting period in California and one witness is required. The license is valid for 90 days.

Colorado

In Colorado, there is no waiting period. While no witnesses are required, some judges, clergy, and other officials may request them. Couples can "self-solemnize" (get married without an officiant). The marriage license is valid for 35 days.

Connecticut

There is no waiting period in Connecticut, and no witnesses are required. The marriage license is valid for 65 days.

Delaware

Delaware has a 24-hour waiting period. Delaware also requires two witnesses for the wedding ceremony. The marriage license expires after 30 days.

District of Columbia

In Washington, D.C., there is no waiting period, no requirement for witnesses, and the marriage license does not expire.

Florida

In Florida, there is a three-day day waiting period. However, residents who can provide documentation showing they completed a state-approved marriage preparation course within the year do not have to wait the three days. For non-residents of the State of Florida, there isn't a waiting period. However, all couples who apply for a marriage license must read the *Family Law Handbook*. Though not required by law, having witnesses is recommended. The marriage license expires after 60 days.

Georgia

In Georgia, you must apply in the same county where the marriage is being performed if you are a non-resident of the state. There is no waiting period and the marriage license is valid for six months. Witnesses are required in some cases (please check with your county registrar).

Hawaii

There is no waiting period for obtaining a marriage license in Hawaii. You must go online and register to apply for a marriage license in Hawaii. You can mail your paperwork back, and officiants can turn in the paperwork to have it expedited. Officiants have to register their status separately in this state.

Idaho

Idaho requires no waiting period and no witnesses. The marriage license does not expire.

Illinois

In Illinois, no witnesses are required but there is a one-day waiting period. The marriage license is valid for 60 days.

Indiana

There is no waiting period in Indiana and witnesses are not required. The marriage license is valid for 60 days.

Iowa

There is a three-day waiting period in Iowa. You must have one witness present with you when applying, and the marriage license is valid for six months.

Kansas

Kansas requires a three-day waiting period and two witnesses at the ceremony. The marriage license is valid for six months.

Kentucky

While there is no waiting period in Kentucky, you are required to have two witnesses at the ceremony. The marriage license is valid for 30 days.

Louisiana

Louisiana has a 24-hour waiting period but that can be waived under special circumstances. Two witnesses are required at the ceremony and the marriage license is valid for 30 days.

Maine

There is no waiting period but two witnesses are required at the ceremony. It's a good idea to check with the municipality for other requirements. The marriage license is valid for 90 days.

Maryland

In Maryland, there is a two-day waiting period. The license must be applied for and picked up in the same county the ceremony is taking place. No witnesses are required and the marriage license is valid for six months.

Massachusetts

Massachusetts has a three-day waiting period; no witnesses are required. The marriage license expires after 60 days.

Michigan

Michigan requires a three-day waiting period (which can be waived in some circumstances) and two witnesses at the ceremony. The marriage license expires after 33 days.

Minnesota

In Minnesota, there is no waiting period and two witnesses are required at the ceremony. The marriage license is valid for six months.

Mississippi

For a couple to obtain a marriage license in Mississippi, both applicants must be 21 years of age or parental consent is required. No witnesses are required and the marriage license does not expire.

Missouri

Missouri does not require a waiting period or witnesses. The marriage license is valid for 30 days.

Montana

Montana has no waiting period and you do not need witnesses. The marriage license expires after 180 days.

Nebraska

In Nebraska, there is no waiting period but two witnesses are required at the ceremony. The marriage license is valid for one year.

Nevada

Nevada has no waiting period but one witness is required at the ceremony. The marriage license is valid for one year.

New Hampshire

There is no waiting period in New Hampshire and witnesses are not required. The marriage license expires after 90 days.

New Jersey

New Jersey requires a three-day waiting period and one witness at the signing of the marriage license who knows both of the parties. The marriage license expires after six months.

New Mexico

New Mexico has no waiting period but requires two witnesses at the ceremony. The marriage license does not expire.

New York

New York requires a one-day waiting period (though it may be waived) and one witness at the wedding ceremony. The marriage license is valid for 60 days.

North Carolina

There is no waiting period in North Carolina, but two witnesses are required at the ceremony. The marriage license is valid for 60 days.

North Dakota

In North Dakota, there is no waiting period, but two witnesses are required at the wedding ceremony. The marriage license is valid for 60 days.

Ohio

Ohio has no waiting period and no witness requirement. The marriage license is valid for 60 days.

Oklahoma

In Oklahoma, there is no waiting period if the applicants are 18 years of age or older. Two witnesses are required at the wedding ceremony. The marriage license is valid for only 10 days.

Oregon

Oregon has a three-day waiting period, but many western counties will waive it with payment of $20 or so, depending on the county. Curry County, by Brookings, Oregon will not waive it. In Oregon, you must go in person to apply and receive the license. The marriage license is valid for 60 days.

Pennsylvania

In Pennsylvania, two types of marriage licenses are issued: a traditional marriage license and a "self-uniting" marriage license, which "does not require an officiant to solemnize the marriage." Pennsylvania has a three-day waiting period with no witnesses required. The marriage license is valid for 60 days.

Rhode Island

There is no waiting period in Rhode Island, but two witnesses are required at the ceremony. The marriage license expires after 90 days.

South Carolina

In South Carolina, witnesses are not required. There is a one-day waiting period. The marriage license does not expire.

South Dakota

There is no waiting period in South Dakota. One witness is required at the ceremony. The marriage license expires after 20 days.

Tennessee

Tennessee does not have a waiting period. Witnesses are not required, but there is room on the license for one witness to sign. The marriage license expires after 30 days.

Texas

Texas has a three-day waiting period. Witnesses are not required. The marriage license expires after 89 days.

Utah

While there is no waiting period in Utah, two witnesses of the ceremony are required. The marriage license expires after 30 days.

Vermont

Vermont has no waiting period and no witnesses are required. The marriage license is valid for 60 days.

Virginia

Virginia has no waiting period and no witnesses are required. The marriage license is valid for 60 days.

Washington

Washington has a three-day waiting period. You can apply online (for example, in King County, where Seattle is located) in order to expedite the process. The marriage license expires after 60 days. Two witnesses are required at the ceremony.

West Virginia

West Virginia has no waiting period and no witnesses are required. The marriage license is valid for 60 days.

Wisconsin

In Wisconsin, there is a six-day waiting period (though it can be waived) and two witnesses are required at the ceremony. The marriage license expires after 30 days.

Wyoming

Wyoming has no waiting period but two witnesses are required at the ceremony. The marriage license expires after one year.

International ceremonies

Planning to elope outside of the U.S.? When it comes to international weddings, there is an added amount of paperwork and scheduling. Each country has different regulations, but it's safe to say that a wedding visa (yes, there is such a thing), a registered date that you're getting married, and in-person clerk appointments might all be required. Wedding visas can normally take several months and have a precise timeline for being submitted. I encourage you to research the country you're considering but don't be surprised if the logistics are more than what you want to go through.

An alternative is having a brief ceremony at home (it can be in your kitchen) and complete the paperwork at your local courthouse. It's infinitely easier. Then you're able to have your symbolic ceremony abroad, before or after the official paperwork is filed.

29

CONCLUSION

We're finally at the end, my friends, which is both sad and exciting. It's sad because our time together has come to a close, but exciting because you have newfound knowledge and inspiration. You have information that can truly change your life if you're willing to take the risk and jump headfirst into the unknown.

While reading this book, you might have laughed, cried, or said, "Yassssssss, this is so true!" You might have done all three, which is a good thing because it means you've taken the time to dig into what you value and who you are. By discovering that it is perfectly okay to speak up for what you want, and to make your own choices for your wedding, you might have recognized that you can take that empowerment and apply it to your life.

You can make your wedding day a unique reflection of you and your spouse-to-be. Not only can you have the wedding day of your dreams, but also you can build the life of your dreams. It didn't dawn on me until I got the idea for this book that the two—eloping for your wedding ceremony and *eloping your life*—are so intimately connected. Eloping is a decision that sets the foundation for your marriage and the rest of your lives together. *Eloping your life* is the same thing. It means creating a life of no regrets, and pursuing your desires, despite other people who express to

you that you are not living up to (their) expectations. It means doing things that are not ordinary, especially things that take you out of your comfort zone. It's about you taking the reins, choosing what works for you, living the life you have dreamt of... so why on Earth not make it phenomenal?

Eloping your life involves a shift in mindset—realizing that you are unique and that there is value in that uniqueness. Shout your passions from the rooftops! It fills me with a sense of awe whenever I meet people who challenge the status quo. A woman who is confident in her skills as an engineer. A man who loves a good romance novel. A woman who accepts her beautiful body that isn't a size 2. A couple who lives an unconventional lifestyle in a tiny home in order to reduce waste. It's really about having the courage to be who you are.

The shifts you make can be simple yet significant. I have a friend who has never felt comfortable taking herself on a solo date. She would want to see a movie, but no one was available to go with her. So she didn't go. Since eloping her life (starting with her elopement), she has realized that she has the power to challenge social norms. According to social norms (such as boys wear blue and girls wear pink), a solo date is "lonely" or "sad." That sentiment about solo dates makes *me* sad. I see solo dates as a mark of independence and strength.

When you elope your life, you challenge what is expected of you. Think about the typical sequence of life's milestones. Finish school, get a job, get married, buy a house, have children. We've been shown by example that there is a generally accepted order to things. But I know many empowered women who have chosen to elope their lives and start a business or buy a home without a partner by their side. They didn't wait for the perfect spouse to come along before creating the life they desired.

For me, eloping my life has meant facing my fears. I have stage fright when I sing, particularly during auditions. It's awful. My hands shake, my throat tightens up, and my singing skills go through the floor. There have been musicals I really wanted to be part of but I missed out because I was too afraid to audition. Ultimately I had to ask myself how invested I was in staying afraid. It was easier than auditioning, sure. But at what cost? If I hadn't eventually faced my fears and auditioned for musicals like "Into the Woods" and "Mamma Mia," I would have missed out on friendships, fits of laughter around a backyard fire, and being part of something I love.

Eloping your life can mean shifts in your lifestyle. Are you tired of working at a job that doesn't fulfill you? Maybe you're thinking, "Well, I have a job and it's secure, so why would I give that up?" but at the same time, you're passionate about a different field. My husband went to school three different times in three different majors before he landed on the job he loves. He is now a home health nurse and is passionate about chronic care, educating families on healthy lifestyles, and end-of-life transitions.

You can "elope" to a completely different lifestyle in a new environment. Someone who lives in the Midwest may be drawn to the Pacific Northwest but face family pressure to stay put. Perhaps you grew up in the city and long for life by the sea. When we choose a life that's different from what our family has chosen, some people take it *very* personally. You may be asked, "What's wrong with what *we've* chosen?" This isn't limited to moving—families are funny that way. I have a friend whose family insists she doesn't have a "real job" because she has worked remotely (from a beach town) since long before working remotely was a common thing to do. It's hard when the people we love don't "get" what we are doing or why. They might not ever fully understand. Remember, your choices are not up for debate. *You are doing you.*

When you elope your life, your daily state of being changes. You might find that you don't compare yourself to others as often as you did before. You could discover that you no longer balk at challenges because you know that if at first you fail, that does not determine your worth.

A product of eloping your life is making changes that make you happier and more fulfilled. Whether it's auditioning for a play, exploring or a new sport, or simply doing something alone as opposed to with a partner (taking yourself on a date, going to a social dance class alone, etc.), you're up for it. Train for that 5k. Switch up that career. Get those hair extensions you're worried will come off as shallow. Say no commitments that mentally or emotionally drain you. Will it always be easy? No. You might be met with skepticism. But will this new approach be worth it? Oh yes.

You will find that by being yourself, you will inspire others to do the same. By accepting and celebrating who you are, you will be a beacon for others.

Now go! Go out there and be unabashedly yourself. I feel like a mama bird ushering her babies out of the nest, and I couldn't be more proud. Be more fulfilled and less burdened by life's expectations. When you realize that there is no competition between you and any other person, you can focus on what fills your cup. Take that new job. Relocate. Take a solo trip somewhere. Start a family, or don't. Learn a new language. Go fall in love with your hobbies and passions. Adopt a dog or a cat (or a bird or a reptile). Say good-bye to tiresome responsibilities, and carve out time for things that you adore. Learn to say no to commitments that don't ignite a spark within you; build boundaries between yourself and people or things that leave you feeling empty. What it all comes down to is the life you want to live can be yours, as long as you don't get in your own way. Make it happen, make waves, and above all...

Elope your life.

P.S.

THIS CHAPTER IS FOR YOU,
MANLY MEN

TK.

Chapter by the Author's husband.

TRUE STORIES

TK.

Six stories from the Author's clients about their elopement.

Sam Starns is an industry leader in adventure elopement photography. After regretting her own traditional wedding, she began her mission to empower individuals to become unapologetically themselves by creating a wedding day and life that they can be uniquely proud of.

With nearly a decade of wedding experience, Starns has traveled to numerous states and countries for elopements to jumpstart the transformation for real change to encourage anyone to become their authentic self.

With a passion for protecting our public lands and love for the outdoors, Starns donates a percentage of services including photography packages and book sales to a nonprofit dedicated to helping preserve public lands.

CPSIA information can be obtained
at www.ICGtesting.com
Printed in the USA
BVHW021158260720
584559BV00001B/2